P9-AQP-473

HOME TO POLAND

Home to Poland

CHRISTINE HOTCHKISS

FARRAR, STRAUS AND CUDAHY, NEW YORK

Fernald Library
Colby Junior College
New London, New Hampshire

DK
441
H6

Copyright © 1958
by Christine Hotchkiss

First Printing, 1958

Library of Congress Catalog Number: 58-7837

The author wishes to make acknowledgment to DeWitt
Wallace, to Lila Acheson Wallace, and to the editors of
Reader's Digest for their encouragement and for the help
that made the trip to Poland possible.

PRINTED IN THE UNITED STATES OF AMERICA
AMERICAN BOOK–STRATFORD PRESS, INC., NEW YORK

39121

Contents

Contents

TO DENISE

CHAPTER 1

"Since October..."

"PASSENGERS for Warsaw to Gate No. 8 for immediate embarkation," the loudspeaker at the Brussels airport suddenly called into space. As we walked toward the plane, I stared at my fellow passengers. They certainly looked quite different from a West European crowd. They were dressed shabbily, men and women bundled up in gray, green fur-trimmed overcoats, and they carried huge cartons of food. I made my way to a seat near the window, next to a large wicker basket overflowing with grapefruits, oranges and bananas, with a few cans of pineapple juice among them. Its owner was a red-cheeked Polish woman in a brown skirt and blue sweater and a warm, colorful scarf tied around her head peasant-fashion. Her name was Yanina, and she came from Grodzisk, near Warsaw. She had just spent two weeks visiting her daughter in Belgium, her first trip abroad in over seventeen years. She enjoyed every minute of it, she said— had bought many nice things which she hoped she could get through the customs. And did I know that almost nobody in Poland had seen a banana or a grapefruit for many years? It was good to have a look at the prosperous world outside, but things had picked up in Poland recently, since October, and she hoped that the change would be permanent.

3

I leaned back in my seat and looked at the wintry clouds below me. I too was going back, but in a different way. I was returning to the land of my birth, my first visit since I had left it as a young girl. Eighteen years had elapsed: a war had run its course, the Russians had taken over, my family had been dispersed, our house was ours no more. Until now I had never had any desire to go back. Married to an American and living in New York, I had become as much a part of Manhattan as any of its other two million transient inhabitants. The Iron Curtain was thick, and behind it lay a forbidding police state with which, I thought, I no longer had anything in common.

That was until one October Sunday in 1956. It was a cold, rainy morning, and I looked forward with pleasure to the familiar thickness of the Sunday New York *Times*, spread in front of me on the table. On the front page, Sydney Gruson's lucid dispatches from Warsaw told an amazing story of a dramatic weekend, of patriotism and great courage, out of which had emerged a new Poland. The Poles' love of freedom had reasserted itself once again, and they had sent the Russians packing.

This was the first powerful strike for freedom in an autumn crowded with historical events.

I was proud of my former countrymen and, though the drama of the Hungarian uprising overshadowed the news from Poland for the next two weeks, I followed events there avidly and was thankful that the country was being saved from the Hungarian holocaust. I searched out Polish friends that I had not seen for years. I wrote to my Congressman, urging him to speed aid to Poland. And then, one day in mid-November, I wrote a memo to my boss at *The Reader's Digest* suggesting that I be sent to Poland—the new Poland. "I grew up there, and know the language," I wrote. "Things have changed in Poland recently. I would like to see for myself. . . ." Next day my trip was okayed.

My husband was less than enthusiastic. He thought the whole idea preposterous and he predicted long, dreary years in Siberia. Quite a few of our friends were equally pessimistic, and for a while I was surrounded by a mood of sympathetic gloom.

It took me over two months to get a visa, but finally it came through.

Now, high up in the air, my thoughts were of home in New York and of Denise, my little girl, who painstakingly located Poland in her first-grade school atlas and remarked it was "very far from New York." My feelings were mixed. I was heading into an adventure; there was no going back, and the clouds yielded no answer.

Four hours later I saw a field of potatoes, a line of ramshackle buildings and a grass-covered runway rushing toward me and we touched down in front of a sign saying WARSZAWA. I stepped out of the plane into the cold, wintry air and followed my companions into a small, dark waiting room, where we sat for some time while our names were called out one by one and our passports duly stamped. A blond girl in a brown, fur-trimmed coat and a white scarf prettily framing her face came up to me and said that she was glad to see I had arrived and that there would be a car to take me to the hotel. She was an official from Orbis, the Polish Intourist, who handle all travel and operate the Bristol, Warsaw's best hotel, reserved for visiting foreigners.

Stepping over large puddles, we followed the porter to a small gray-black car, the Polish Warszawa, copied after the popular Russian Pobeda model. We drove through gray empty streets and passed dilapidated buildings and a long stretch of ruins. It was getting dark, but all the time I was straining, trying to recognize a familiar landmark or a street.

But I remembered nothing; it all looked strange, war-torn and very poor.

We had just rounded a corner, and out of the grayish mist there emerged a vista that suddenly looked familiar. There was a park on the left. It was the Saski Gardens, I was sure; only some of the columns were missing, and the equestrian statue of Prince Joseph Poniatowski, the favorite hero of my childhood, did not seem to be there any more.

"What happened to Poniatowski?" I asked the driver.

"He was moved to Lazienki Park during the reconstruction of the square. He's all right, just as handsome as ever."

Now I knew where we were. We would soon be turning into the Krakowskie Przedmiescie, Warsaw's Fifth Avenue, and the Bristol would be there, on the left. In my memory it was splendid and glamorous. As a child I had sometimes accompanied my parents on a brief visit to Warsaw from the country place where we lived. I remembered the excitement I felt each time we pulled in front of the Bristol. I loved its majestic, blue-carpeted lobby, the red plush curtains, the profusion of flowers and the cheerful, bowing attendants. It was a particular thrill to eat in the main dining room with the orchestra playing Viennese waltzes. The first ball I ever went to in my life was a charity dance in the raspberry-colored ballroom of the Bristol. It took place six months before the outbreak of war and it was the last ball that was ever held there. Owned by the Association of Landowners, of which my father was once president, the hotel was run to perfection. It had suffered relatively minor damage during the war and was used as headquarters, first by the Germans and then by the Russians after the war.

The car came to a stop and I jumped out eagerly. The red armchairs were still there in the hotel hall, but they now looked almost black with the years. Gone were the glass chandeliers and the luxurious blue carpets, and the hydrangeas in pots, behind which we used to hide from our nurse. There were a few dusty palms. A bulb in a bright yellow shade threw a harsh, glaring light from the ceiling. The far corners were dark, filled with shadowy forms of people busily talking and shaking hands.

An Orbis girl with a Max Factor make-up glanced at my shoes with approval and handed me a key to my room. Up we went in a creaking glass elevator, and I wondered whether the old man who ran it had been there since the war. He wore a faded blue uniform, and his kind, wrinkled face looked familiar. He carried my bags to my room, and when I gave him a tip and thanked him he bent low and kissed my hand in the best feudal tradition. Later I asked him his name and how long he had been there. He told me that until the war he used to be the room clerk at the Europejski Hotel across the Square from the Bristol. The Germans deported him for forced labor; he came back and fought in the Warsaw uprising, during which the Europejski was burned down. He was now the *bagazowy* (bell boy) at the Bristol. He beamed when I told him who I was; he remembered my father quite well and many of his friends. During my stay in Warsaw I had many long chats with old Piotr. They took me all the way back to my childhood.

My room had a table in the middle with four straight chairs around it. The small bed with a quilt buttoned into the top sheet was in one corner, while the rest of the room was taken up by a large yellow wardrobe with doors that would never stay shut. A lamp with an old-fashioned green shade came straight down from the ceiling. The telephone was at the opposite end of the room, as far away from the bed as possible. But the window was wide, and in the gray winter dusk the baroque outline of the lovely Wizytki Church gleamed faintly across the little park opposite. Behind it, down the steep, sandy embankment, flowed the Vistula.

I was back in Warsaw. It seemed strange and unreal.

One of the first things that struck me when I looked around the hotel that evening was the general feeling of lightness and casual informality in the air. People talked and laughed loudly. The two coffee rooms on the mezzanine were full, the telephone booths were crowded. Floor maids were rushing around in a helpful but disorganized fashion. Though the Bristol was dingy, badly in need of a coat of paint and some scrubbing, there was none of the depressing atmosphere of discreet scrutiny peculiar to a police state. I had expected to be checked and watched and surveyed by many pairs of eyes. But no one bothered about me.

"Are there any microphones in the rooms?" I asked a Polish newspaperman who had come to say hello on my arrival. I was half serious and did not really expect an answer.

"You must know," he said earnestly, "that there was quite a change in October. Now we can all say what we like. This is Poland again. You should have been here last year at this time. Then you could tell the difference."

"*Since October.*" I was to hear this phrase over and over again.

There were two dining rooms at the Bristol—both drafty and badly lit. Dozens of waiters seemed to be hovering around, but the service was unbelievably slow.

"Liaison between the kitchen and the dining room does not exist in this place," a British military man tersely remarked, storming out.

After many meals at the Bristol I came to the conclusion that the fault lay with the socialist system of employing too many waiters and eliminating the custom of tips. It took the incentive out of the waiters' jobs.

The dining room that night was half empty. Few Poles can afford Bristol prices. Those who can, such as writers who in Communist countries are well off and high government officials, come in late. Poles usually lunch at three, have dinner at nine-thirty or later.

I sat down at a small table as far away from the drafty window as possible. I could see the grayish-white cotton curtains rise up and down with the draft. The menu was a long one, most of it written by hand and in Polish. I decided on a cup of hot borscht with *pasztecik* (a beet soup with a meat-filled pancake) and cutlets Pozarski to follow.

I was joined at the table by Gabriel Reiner, the jovial, round-faced head of the Cosmos Travel Bureau in New York. Mr. Reiner was born in Polish Lithuania and speaks Polish, Russian and a dozen other languages. Only two days before his arrival the artificially high rate of exchange of the zloty had been revised to bring it into line with Western currencies. Instead of the former exchange of four zlotys to the dollar, an exchange which was based on the Russian ruble, it was now twenty-four to the dollar—still high, but a step forward and an advantage to visitors. It now cost only one dollar for a breakfast of ersatz coffee and rolls, instead of the former six dollars.

I asked Mr. Reiner whether he had been instrumental in bringing down the rate of exchange.

"No," he said, "this is one more sign of Poland's desire to resume contacts with the West. The former rate was prohibitive and totally unrealistic. It will of course have an initial adverse impact on their imports, but as far as tourism is concerned we can at last begin to talk business. Thousands of Americans of Polish origin would like to come over to Poland for a visit, but the delay on visas is too long and the prices have been out of line until lately."

He was in the process of negotiating an agreement with Orbis, hopeful that travel between America and Poland would increase.

A small, tired-looking man with a sad, kindly face came to

greet Mr. Reiner. He was an official of the Polish Shipping
Line, State-owned and State-managed. He had recently been
transferred to Warsaw from the Polish port of Gdynia on the
Baltic. He suggested that we have a *jarzebiak*—a variation of
vodka, made of bitter-sweet berries—with him.

"How are things in the shipping circles, Mr. Bielecki?"
asked Reiner. "Hope you are getting ready to receive large
waves of American tourists and that you are beginning to
streamline your procedures. You will soon be competing for
Western business."

Bielecki looked even sadder than before and shrugged his
shoulders in dismay. "Not until we fire all the deadwood," he
announced. "You see, in a socialist state full employment is a
basic principle. As a result, our offices are filled with inefficient do-nothings. There are at least four people to do a
job that in your economy is easily handled by one well-
trained employee. I know; I worked in Chicago for three
years. Our overemployment creates constant roadblocks. No
use telling people to stay home, draw their pay, but refrain
from coming to the office. Their living conditions are so dismal that the office becomes a welcome haven. Many got
their jobs under the previous regime, but even so, there is no
way to fire them. The situation may improve in the future,
now that some ministries are being disbanded and the machinery of the State is being progressively cut down."

"Where do you live, Mr. Bielecki?" I asked.

His faded blue eyes reddened, and he made a desperate
move with his hands. "For eight months," he replied, "I have
been trying to locate quarters here for my wife and three
children. But it is impossible, quite hopeless. I left them in
Gdynia when I moved. There was no other way to do it.
They are still there, and this separate life may continue in-
definitely. I have seen them only once since I left; I went
there for a day and a half when our last baby was born. I

don't expect to see them again until I get my annual vacation
sometime in the latter part of this year. In the meantime I
have a small bed and a table in a room which I share with
three men. One of the men plays the accordion in a band
and is likely to come home at all hours. I dislike going back
there at night."

He went off with Mr. Reiner to discuss business in the adjoining coffee shop. In spite of the very late hour, it was
filled. I could see why the inhabitants of Warsaw liked to
stay up in the evenings; the *kawiarnias* (coffee shops) were
gayer and more congenial than most homes.

I retrieved my key from the smiling room clerk. She was a
good-looking woman in her early thirties, carefully made up
and dressed in an American-made nylon sweater. It was given
to her by one of the hotel guests, she told me. She asked about
American fashions at great length and inquired whether I
had brought *Vogue* or *Harper's Bazaar* in my luggage. I
promised to send her some from New York.

It was well past midnight when I slowly went up to my
room. The day had been a long one.

When I woke up the next morning the Square across from
the hotel was white and the Wizytki Church wore a blanket
of snow. A bitter wind from the great Eastern plains rattled
the loose-fitting windows of my room. I dressed warmly and
went out to see what the new Warsaw looked like. Twelve
years before, the city had been completely destroyed by the
Germans. It had been rebuilt brick by brick under the Communist regime.

Warsaw is built along the banks of the Vistula River. The
center of town and its main residential districts lie on the left,
on the western banks of the river. Praga, the industrial suburb, and the newest housing development of Saska Kepa are
on the right, the eastern bank. Warsaw's main thoroughfare,

which traverses the city from north to south, parallel to the river, is the Krakowskie Przedmiescie (Krakow suburb), a handsome, wide avenue lined with historic old houses. Farther south its name changes to Nowy Swiat (the New World), then to Aleje Ujazdowskie (the Riding Alley), a tree-lined avenue where most of Warsaw's elite used to live. Nowy Swiat and the Krakowskie Przedmiescie, where the Bristol Hotel is located, were Warsaw's main shopping centers and the first streets to be completely rebuilt since the war. North of them is Stare Miasto (the Old City), a picturesque maze of narrow, winding streets lined by colorful 17th-century Flemish-style merchants' houses reconstructed from old plans. The East-West Highway, a modern, daringly designed thoroughfare, connects the Stare Miasto with the suburb of Praga on the eastern bank of the river. To the left is Muranow, a desert expanse of stone, where new residential houses are rising on the ruins of the former ghetto. Until recently, only death stalked the eerie expanse of ruins, where more than a million Jews were inhumanly destroyed by the Nazis.

Standing in front of the Bristol, I looked at the streets I knew well. They were quiet; there was hardly any traffic. An occasional car or a horse-driven fiacre slid by quietly in the snow. The façade of the house opposite was pocked with shell marks; the impact of the war was visible all around. There were plenty of people on the sidewalks. Bundled up in fleece-lined overcoats, they walked swiftly ahead without looking about. Almost everyone carried some heavy paper-wrapped package. All looked busy and intent on a purpose. I soon learned that the struggle to survive was their worry.

A few blocks down toward Nowy Swiat people were queueing in front of a grocery store. They stood out in the cold, occasionally stomping their feet, the long waiting line profiled against the graceful outline of an 18th-century palace freshly rebuilt since the war. A slim girl wearing ski pants

and heavy boots said that a shipment of Krakow sausage had
arrived at the shop in the morning. She was not yet certain
the rumor was true, but it was worth looking into. The
Krakow sausage is a special type—round, brown, very dry; a
delicacy with the dark-rye Polish bread and with beer. The
girl talked to me casually. Her attention was focused on the
head of the line, slowly moving into the door of the shop
under the colonnaded arcade.

Beyond us stretched Nowy Swiat. It was a lovely street—
long, narrow and slightly arched, lined with ivory-colored
brick plaster houses two to three stories high, with delicately
suspended ironwork balconies. The houses had inner court-
yards planted with trees. The upper stories were lived in;
small shops occupied the street level. The wares in the windows were dingy: artificial, sickly pink underwear, dull-col-
ored woolens, kitchenware made of cheap grayish enamel—
all products of the various State-owned coöperatives. People
hurried past them indifferently.

Now and then, over a millinery shop or a shoemaker's window half hidden in a courtyard, the owner's name appeared
in bold print. It was easy to tell such a shop from the distance.
The display was harmonious, the goods were expensive but
looked nice; tight groups of people surrounded it, pressing
toward the small window. This was private initiative which
had been slowly rearing its head since October.

I squeezed in to press with the others. The tag on the pair
of black pumps made of heavy-grained leather said 950 zl.—
$40 at the official exchange, around $9 according to the black-
market quotation—a fair monthly salary for many Poles. The
brown furry felt hat next door was 400 zlotys—half a month's
salary for some. "Copied from the 1957 Paris collections,"
said the penciled note over it. It looked both encouraging and
pathetic. The felt was stiff and unwieldy, but a year ago such
a sign would not have appeared on Nowy Swiat. The shop

next door was a DESA, a State-owned coöperative, where people brought pictures, rare china and valuable carpets to sell. The State charged a 20 percent commission to the owner. A fine snowy landscape by Falat, a 19th-century Polish painter, was propped in the middle of the window. The tag on it was 2000 zlotys, the price of about three pairs of medium-quality shoes.

I walked past the baroque Church of the Holy Cross, topped by a gigantic statue of Christ with a cross. It too had been rebuilt since the war, the statue brought back from Germany where it had been taken for scrap. Chopin's heart lay inside the church, near the altar, in a gold-lined jeweled box.

The lovely street ended abruptly at a wide, busy thorough-fare which cut Nowy Swiat east and west. This was Aleje Jerozolimskie (Jerusalem Alley), a busy, commercial artery. A huge pile of gray stone masonry rose arrogantly on my left. It was a modern structure, lavishly trimmed with black marble, with a wide, semicircular parking space filled with black Chevrolets and Mercedes. It looked incongruous and foreign, silhouetted against the classic façade of the National Museum behind it and the line of old houses marking the approach to the river.

"What is this?" I asked a group of three boys standing in front of a cigar store, reading the newspaper headlines.

"The headquarters of the Central Committee," said one, a pale, lanky boy of about 18. "It would make a wonderful hotel, don't you think?" he added, with a quick, mocking grin.

This was Warsaw all over. No matter what the conditions, the inhabitants' humor keeps on. I had yet to see the Palace of Culture, the Soviet Union's magnanimous gift to the Poles, and hear all the jokes it gave rise to.

I turned back into Nowy Swiat, wanting to see more of it.

The vast panorama of Warsaw's historical buildings now stretched in front of me to the north. There was the Palace of Staszyc, with the Copernicus statue in front of it; the Potocki Palace, where the Ministry of Culture is located; the Warsaw University, with its fine wrought-iron heavy gates; the Radziwill and the Lubomirski Palaces, yellow-tinted 18th-century structures, which used to house Polish nobles, now faithfully reconstructed according to the smallest details. Most of the familiar landmarks were there. Even the old barrel-shaped house at the corner of the Street of the Senators was still there, but it now looked different, newly painted; the patina of the centuries had been lost somewhere in the careful restoration process. The Branicki House was there, too, just the same, but not quite, because it never used to have a garden in front. Most of the elements in the view were real, but transposed, slightly altered, such as we find them in dreams. The houses of yesterday had gardens added to them—new walls, new façades, new vistas. The sensation created was baffling.

Warsaw has been Poland's capital for the last 400 years, ever since the 16th century, when the residence of the Polish kings was moved there from the old medieval city of Krakow. In the course of the last 300 years it was destroyed many times by successive Swedish, German, Austrian and Russian attacks; each time it was quickly rebuilt. In the fall of 1944, at the time of the ill-fated Warsaw uprising, the whole town was razed to the ground. German SS detachments went from street to street, dynamiting the houses which had escaped fire or artillery shelling. A town of over a million inhabitants became a desert of rubble and smoking ruins.

"This city will not rise again," said the German Commander von dem Bach.

He was wrong.

A great feeling of love bound the people of Warsaw close

to their capital. During the severe winter that followed, crowds of bedraggled people converged on the town from all sides. They came in horse-driven carts, in old broken-down lorries, on bicycles and on foot, dragging sleighs behind them with remnants of miserable belongings. They gazed at the ruins of their city, their faces wet with the snow and with tears.

Each week the numbers of returning exiles grew larger. Tens of thousands came back and remained stubbornly, though the reality they faced was worse than the most nightmarish dream. There was no drinking water, no light, no food, no communication of any sort. And, worst of all, there were mines—mines laid down treacherously by the withdrawing Germans in streets and on squares and in the cellars of the houses that escaped total destruction.

Reconstruction work was started immediately by people still living in cellars, clinging to every remnant that was left. They boarded up broken windows with planks; with hand shovels and picks they removed the accumulated rubble, loading it on rickety horse-carts. In a few weeks, walking communication between the streets was restored and water wells opened for use. Each day processions of people with buckets lined in front of them in the cold.

The task of rebuilding the city went on with the help of women and high-school youths. According to official statistics, more than twenty million metric tons of rubble were removed and turned into building material. During the first three years of rebuilding, 100 carloads of rubble were taken out of the city every day. "About 100,000 carloads in all," one of the architects told me. "Enough to build a pyramid 100 miles square and about 180 miles tall," he said, laughing.

Slowly Warsaw began to rise from the ashes. But about the same time a subtle change took place in the city's construction plans. The Communist Government, which had taken control of Poland on the heels of the Red Army, had a difficult decision to make: should they build houses for people, thousands and thousands of them, forgetting about everything else; or should they rebuild the old Warsaw in its fine historical frame, turn palaces into ministries and take credit before history for the gigantic task of reconstruction?

It was quickly decided that the common man could wait for his living quarters. The reconstruction of offices, ministries and historical buildings was given priority. It was a decision that no capitalist government, given similar circumstances, would have ever dared adopt.

Meticulous care was taken to follow authentic designs, to re-erect exactly the classic 17th-century houses of the old city, the lovely baroque churches for which Warsaw was famous and the Renaissance palaces of the Polish nobility where Communist ministries were installed. Canaletto's paintings of 18th-century Warsaw scenes, saved from the burning ruins of the former Royal Castle, served as architectural models from which detailed ornaments on the buildings were copied.

Looking around at the handsome houses, their graceful shapes rising softly in the whirling snowflakes, one had to admit that the Communist Government had done a good reconstruction job. They had restored the monuments, the palaces and the gardens to house the Communist officials and had given them lovely vistas to look at. That the ordinary citizen, to whom a paradise had been promised, was still living three and four to a room, did not worry the socialist planners. Warsaw was well on the way to becoming a beautiful city, and history would give them credit for it—so they hoped.

CHAPTER 2

Old Friends in a New Society

THE *kawiarnia* Nowy Swiat was crowded. In the deep window-seats covered with vivid red plush, couples sat close together holding hands and whispering softly over endless cups of black coffee. Women in perky hats and bright scarves clustered around marble-top tables in the middle, laughed gaily, gossiped hard, looked around now and then to see if anyone they knew was arriving. They consumed quantities of small cakes topped with whipped cream. No matter how unavailable food became, there always seemed to be an abundance of cakes in Warsaw. Groups of men talked intently, emphasizing a particular point with a gesture; some sat buried in newspapers, half hidden in clouds of cigarette smoke. Acquaintances were formally acknowledged with deep bows; greeting kisses were applied to flirtatiously extended feminine hands; there were smiles, bursts of laughter and heated arguments. The room was warm and alive, astir with sensuality, politics and quick gossip. These were the same people who, during the day, had moved listlessly in the streets. Here they were animated and vibrant, enjoying their favorite pastime, the great Central European institution, the *kawiarnia*. No one here was in a hurry to be waited on or to leave. One could spend a whole day, if one wished, over a small cup of

black coffee, glancing at a succession of newspapers mounted
on long, wooden sticks. It was hard to find a free table because many occupants had been sitting there since morning.

I was to meet Roman in the first room—the one with the
surrealistic paintings, he had said.

Roman was a friend of the family, some ten years older
than I. He had been a rising star in the firmament of prewar
Poland: at the age of twenty-eight he was one of the country's youngest and most respected economists. He was des-
tined for a brilliant future, but the war nipped his promising
career in the bud. I did not see much of him during the war;
he spent years with a Polish mission in Beirut in the Middle
East. A mutual friend had told me that he was now back in
Warsaw working on the Economic Council, his old ground.
I called him on the telephone one morning; a visitor from
the moon would not have surprised him more.

I saw him from a distance, looking attentively around, wondering whether he would still recognize me; it had been well
over sixteen years since our last meeting in Paris. Tall, broad
shouldered, with thick blond hair growing far behind a bulging forehead, he had slanting blue eyes and a babyish pink
complexion; his face was a mixture of Nordic and Asiatic
strains. He had been born in Moldavia, the eastern part of
Rumania; and, as my mother remarked, "Anything is likely
to happen in Moldavia." He had always been an exceedingly
odd-looking man, gifted with great personal charm and with
brains. I watched him adjust his tie in the mirror. He was
dressed in a well-cut grayish suit and moved about with assurance. He turned around as I stopped, and we exchanged
warm handshakes, then rushed to get a table which was being
miraculously vacated.

"You look better than you did sixteen years ago," he said,
examining me very closely. "You were too fat, then, and old-

fashioned. You are a complete Westerner now, but your Polish has remained quite good."

Stirring the slowly melting sugar in our teaglasses, we talked of the postwar years. Roman had fought in the Middle East, had been posted to Beirut for two years, then went to Persia to help with the repatriation of Poles deported by Russia in the first year and a half of the war. As it did to thousands of other Poles, V-Day confronted him with a dilemma: should he return to Poland, which by then had a Communist Government directed and controlled by Moscow, or should he become an expatriate and face an uncertain future in the West?

He chose to return. But he did not stay long. The Communist Government looked on him as a spy; his record had been tainted, he was told, by his service with the French and the British. There was no place for people like him. He got out just a step ahead of prison. He then lived in Paris for some years, waiting for conditions to change. But Poland drew him like a magnet. He tried again in the summer of 1956; this time he came back for good. It was safe. His job on the Council was connected with Poland's expanding trade with the West. It was a good sector for him; he brought to it vast experience and an infectious enthusiasm for Western ideas and trade methods.

We talked about his family and his work, about Poland's political situation and about our many friends in common. In his plans for the future an apartment figured as the high-priority target. They were building bachelor's quarters on Marszalkowska Street, he told me; he hoped to get a one-room-and-bath unit there before summer.

"Are you glad you returned?" I asked after we had talked for a long time.

"Yes I am, in spite of the uncertainty of it all," he said. "This is a powder keg, and it may blow up on us at any time,

but Poland is where I belong. Poles who have close ties with
the West should return to government positions and help to
sway the still-vacillating balance. The post-October changes
are endangered because of our lack of new cadres. The majority of our leaders have never been to the West. They
know little about the United States, except what they've been
told by the Russians. It is an important factor which your
people are inclined to discount."

The smoke in the *kawiarnia* was growing dense. "Come,"
said Roman, pushing aside the glass of tea at his elbow, "let's
walk to Lazienki Park. It has stopped snowing."

We walked down Nowy Swiat, stopping at the private-
enterprise shops that were now cropping up every day. There
were new shoe stores and fur shops, dry-goods stores, millinery, jewel and pottery shops with small artistically arranged displays. One store, larger than the others, featured
a multitude of U. S. goods, imported through the PKO, a
State enterprise, in exchange for dollar remittances from relatives in the United States. The shop window was a jumble
of American fountain pens, razor blades, instant-coffee,
playing cards, alarm clocks, lipsticks and fingernail polish.

"Look at private initiative taking over our socialist country!" Roman pointed out with a chuckle. "This is capitalism
at its most rudimentary caveman level. A person will get a
package from relatives somewhere in the United States: he
will keep a few things for himself and resell the rest at a
profit. Razors are in particular demand; as Polish blades can
be used only once, people think it's good economy to pay
higher prices for American or English blades they can use
over and over again. These private shops were supposed to
supplement the State network; but with the general scarcity
of materials on the market, many of them have become private commission stores, selling only imported articles at high
prices. It will all get straightened out in time, when more

consumer goods start flowing into our economy. In the meantime an opening for private initiative has been made. Remember, it is only three months since October."

How could I ever forget this!

We passed the Aleje Jerozolimskie and the Place of the Three Crosses and came down to Lazienki, which is Warsaw's most beautiful park. The majestic old trees formed a stately wide avenue which led to a jewel-like little white palace—the summer theater built by Poland's last King Stanislaw August. In front of it was a round lake, the scene of my first skating lesson.

I saw the equestrian statue I had been looking for near the Bristol. Prince Joseph Poniatowski, known in his days as "Prince Pepi," was King Stanislaw's handsome nephew. He was a soldier, a statesman, a writer—the most dashing man of his era. No historian ever attempted to record the list of his loves and adventures. He was beloved by all women, but could be faithful to none. He put his trust in Napoleon, who promised to restore independence to Poland. At the head of the Polish Lancers he served the French Emperor for six long, faithful years. He covered Napoleon's retreat from Leipzig, and was shot by the Prussian artillery while crossing the River Elster on a white horse in midstream. His lifelike granite statue by the famous Danish sculptor Thorwaldsen stood in front of us now, framed by snow-covered trees.

"I suppose that if Prince Pepi were alive today he would probably vote for Gomulka," I said hesitantly.

"Most of his family and descendants did last January," said Roman.

One afternoon a small, blond woman, with a fresh open face and a very energetic manner, came into my room at the Bristol. Her beige fleece-lined coat, rubber-soled sport shoes and the small feathered hat gingerly tilted to one side

accentuated her businesslike personality. We used to know
each other when we were children. Anka was a distant cousin.
"My family are very anxious to meet you," she said briskly.
"You might as well see how people in Poland live these days.
Let's go."

I remembered that even as a child I was always bossed by
Anka. We were about the same age, but she had always
assumed the initiative in our games. She had remained in Poland through the war, married an architect and was now living in Warsaw with her husband and two boys. I had written
her a post card to say that I would like to see her. She arrived
the next morning, unastonished, matter-of-factly, as if we
had just seen each other last week.

"I am not at all surprised to see you," she announced.
"Lots of people have come here since October, and I thought
you might be turning up someday soon. Good thing you did
not arrive a year earlier. I would have had to pretend that I
had never received your post card; it would have been quite
impossible to see you. Now all this has changed, luckily. We
look forward to having you in our house."

She had very large, round, brown eyes, high cheekbones
and blond hair tightly drawn in a bun. Her vitality seemed
to have increased with the years.

We got into a *dorozka* (horse fiacre) as there were no
taxis anywhere; there are only about sixty of them in Warsaw. The rickety old horse made slow progress against the
sting of the gusty February wind, in spite of the shouted en-
couragements of the driver. I pulled an old moth-eaten rug
from the bottom of the cab. "Don't put it on your knees!"
shouted Anka. "It's probably full of fleas." I let it drop.

We went down Nowy Swiat, past the Church of the Holy
Cross, and turned right into Marszalkowska Street. We
stopped in front of a gray stone apartment house next to a
State-owned china shop. We climbed four flights of stairs.

There were five name tablets pinned on the heavy oak door of the apartment on the left.

"You see all the co-tenants?" asked Anka. "The apartment has exactly six rooms, plus one kitchen and one toilet with bath. Five families live in it. The only tenant with two rooms is a newspaperman with three children; he's got lots of space."

The passage was dark and smelled musty. Anka opened a door on the right, and we came into a large room painted a vivid shade of sky blue. It was light because of two old-fashioned high windows looking over Marszalkowska Street. There was a round table with chairs in the middle, bright Oriental rugs on the floor and two sofa beds in the corner with lots of multicolored pillows on them. A fine English table at one end contrasted with a common clothes rack next to it. There were family photographs, green potted plants and Dresden figurines in the room. Every inch of space had been taken advantage of. It was cramped, but the room had a warm homelike atmosphere. On the radiator cover between the windows stood a silver tea samovar; I had not seen one for years.

Gustaw, Anka's husband, rose from the deep armchair, where he had been reading the *Express Wieczorny* (Evening Express). He was of medium height, stocky, with graying dark hair and a quiet, intelligent face. He and Anka had met during the war at a students' rally at the time of the German occupation. Gustaw was now employed by the Warsaw Municipal Council.

We had tea with lemon in tall glasses with metal holders, and talked about living conditions in Warsaw. As an architect, Gustaw was fairly well off. He received about 6000 zlotys a month—$250 at the official rate of exchange, about $40 at the black-market rate. The rent on the apartment was low; they paid 150 zlotys for it—about a dollar a month at the unofficial rate, $6.25 at the official rate. They spent about

3000 zlotys a month on food for their family of four. The rest went on clothing and an occasional movie or concert. Gustaw had one month's vacation a year; he usually took it in summer at one of the government-run hostels in the mountains or at the seaside. For a small extra charge he could take his family with him. They usually went to Zakopane, a place in the Polish High Tatras. It was a very inexpensive and pleasant way to spend a holiday. "*Wczasy* (paid vacations) are the only good thing the socialist system has produced," said Anka, "except that getting there on the crowded trains is a nightmare. Families get a better deal than single people, who are crowded ten and twelve to a room.

"Do you remember the trip that we took together that last summer?" asked Anka.

It was the summer before the war. We had mapped out a list of houses belonging to relatives and close friends within a forty-mile radius from my home and we set off on horseback to visit them one by one. Anka and I had a wonderful time, stopping a few days in each place. We even won a tennis match, playing jointly against our two older cousins. We took care of our horses ourselves and let no strange stable boy come near them.

"I can still see your brother," said Anka, "as he came to meet us that day, his short little legs across the fat belly of his pony. Poor Yas, he was such an intensely happy young being." My brother Ian had died at sixteen, while fighting in the Warsaw uprising.

Unlike most of her friends, Anka did not have a full-time job. She took care of the house and spent a lot of her time marketing. She often shopped for her friends who had jobs and could not stand in line for meat or butter, which had always been scarce. She also had a part-time job—"trading in rags," she called it.

"You see," she explained, "lots of people around here re-

ceive packages from America. Ever since the duties were
lowered last November, as many as three packages a month
arrive for some families. Most of them are anxious to resell
the contents as soon as possible, in order to buy food or coal
for the winter. Many lack the time to look around and shop
for the best purchaser. I do it for them. I resell medicines to
the State-run pharmacies and get good prices for rare drugs;
penicillin and aureomycin are worth their weight in gold
here. I take American cosmetics to private dealers that I know,
who quickly resell them at a profit. An American lipstick is
worth about 450 zlotys, if the make is well known. There is
a rag market in Warsaw. We call it '*Ciuchy*' (The Rags). I
am going to take you there one day. It's where all the smart
women of Warsaw get their clothes; they all come from
America. I take the contents of one package and return with
the money; then I charge a flat ten percent for my services
and have a lot of fun in the process."

She was bursting with energy. I could see how she could
do well in this business.

Gustaw offered me a Chinese cigarette from a pack resem-
bling the American brands. It had a strange, sweetish taste,
unlike any cigarette I had ever tasted. It was not unpleasant,
rather soothing. "They are milder than the Russian," he said,
"better than our own Polish ones—not so strong. People say
they contain opium. I find them satisfying. They are inexpensive and well packed."

During my stay in Poland I was to see these Chinese
cigarettes everywhere, arriving from Chung-King in large
planeloads. They outsold Polish brands three to one.

"Where do the boys sleep?" I asked, looking around the
room for more beds.

Anka opened the door to a biggish closet which had a small
window in it overlooking a courtyard. Two wooden bunks
were suspended on each side of the closet. "We leave the

door open all night so as to give them some air," she explained. "They store the clothes under their beds in two
chests. The boys are taught to be tidy, but it is difficult.
Living quarters are our biggest problem. There seems to be
little hope for improvement in any foreseeable future."

"Still, we are much better off than most people," said Gustaw. "I have a good job that I like. I may eventually get up to
7000 or more zlotys a month. The bare minimum to exist,
if you have one or two children, is about 3500 zlotys a month.
The average worker makes about 1500 a month. If the wife
does not have a job, they go hungry."

Anka and Gustaw's sons came into the room. They had
been skating at a nearby rink. Richard was eight, dark and
round-faced like his father; Adas, aged ten, looked exactly
like Anka. They clicked their heels smartly and kissed my
hand, then proceeded to ask me what kind of car I had in
New York.

"How fast does an American car run?" asked Adas, his blue
eyes twinkling with excitement. "It must be at least two hundred miles an hour! That's what some older boys told us at
the skating rink the other day. They had heard it over the
radio, so it must be true. You should have brought one with
you when you came."

It was now nearly 7 P.M., Anka's allotted time for the use
of the kitchen. She had forty-five minutes to prepare supper
for the family. In the room, in the space between the double
windows, she stored butter, meat, fat and other perishable
items. There was no refrigerator in the house. I went with her
to the kitchen, which was dark with an old-fashioned gas
stove with three burners. An old woman with untidy gray
hair was stirring a soup in a kettle.

"That's old Mrs. Yanowska," whispered Anka. "She takes
care of the Yanowski children while the parents both work.
She has the use of the kitchen before me, but she is always

late with her cooking. Mrs. Yanowska is very untidy, and I always have to clean after her."

Gustaw walked with me to the Bristol. We turned into Swietokrzyska Street, which was all torn up and dimly lighted. There was almost no traffic, and we walked in the middle of the street. It had started to snow. All around us people were hurrying in the darkness. Practically every person had a bundle of some sort under his arm. Men carried bulging brief cases.

"Those with jobs don't have much time to shop," explained Gustaw. "They dash out of the office when they hear the butcher next door has meat. So they carry the day's purchases with them. It makes it hard to travel on a crowded streetcar."

At the corner of Nowy Swiat two young people were bidding good-by to each other. The boy, pale and lanky, raised the collar of his windbreaker and, waving the girl a quick farewell, rushed toward an oncoming streetcar. I did not see how he could possibly get on it.

It was packed solid inside, and there were dozens of people hanging on the steps, on the platform, precariously balanced on one foot or holding uncertainly to a neighbor. A man suspended on the bottom step moved a little, leaving the boy an inch and a half of space on which to balance his left foot. The rest of him hung outside. The old streetcar started off rapidly, and it looked as if the boy would fall and be crushed by the oncoming traffic.

"Nice riding, isn't it?" asked Gustaw, laughing. "We call them bunches of grapes. Everybody in Warsaw travels this way. It is particularly hard on the women, as most of their buttons get torn off. Last night I had a pound of butter flattened onto my chest by a neighbor. Anka still has not succeeded in getting the grease out of the material. We have no dry cleaners in Warsaw, so it gets to be quite a problem with those of us who only have one or two suits to our name."

All the way back, in the soft gaslight of the street, trams and buses clanged rapidly past the graceful 18th-century houses, carrying their cargo of modern-day "human grapes." They took on more people at each stop. I was used to the New York rush-hour crowds, but this was ten times as bad. Still, the passengers did not seem to mind it. They joked, laughed, pushed aside whenever an inch of space became free.

How do they stand it, day after day, I wondered, living three or four to a room, fighting for the simplest commodities—and how do they remain so cheerful?

CHAPTER 3

The Historic Weekend

"Two things amaze me in this country," remarked a French newspaperman in Warsaw, "the incredible freedom of speech these people are allowed to enjoy and their overwhelming poverty."

The very first thing that strikes a new arrival to Poland is the complete, almost belligerent freedom with which people talk and behave. It is so extraordinary for a Communist country that it took me some time to grasp the full meaning of it. The people feel free. They say what they like, criticize the government loudly, crack jokes about Soviet Russia, Communism and at Lenin. They speak their minds on the telephone, and nobody whispers in the crowded cafés and restaurants. The specter of the secret police disappeared in October, and everyone was quick to take advantage of the new freedom.

When I arrived in Poland in February, 1957, the press also was free. All papers, including official government publications, wrote what they pleased. Many attacked Russia bitterly, questioning some of the basic tenets of Communism. They blamed the years of Stalinist rule for the acute poverty the country found itself in. Often I thought there was too much biting criticism of the many phases of government mismanagement and not enough new, constructive ideas.

In time the press was curtailed. Its full-throated song was too much for the sensitive Russian neighbor, who threatened to cut off deliveries of cotton and ore, without which the Polish economy would collapse.

But no one dared to tamper with freedom of speech.

"Do you know the story of the two dogs who met crossing the Polish-Czech frontier?" asked Leszek, a 22-year-old student of the Warsaw University.

We were sitting in the crowded cafeteria of the 300-year-old Warsaw University, eating a lunch of borscht and potatoes. The room was drafty and cold. Around us, along bare wooden tables, sat groups of young people eating fast and talking intently between mouthfuls.

Leszek was frail, dark-haired, with small hands and a pale, highly strung, sensitive face. At that particular moment he was laughing, and his voice was mocking and strong. "The Polish dog said, 'I am going to Prague in order to buy my wife a pair of your fine Czech shoes.'

"The Czech dog looked over his shoulder and said, 'I am crossing into Poland in order to bark.' "

A pretty girl in a green woolen skirt joined us.

"You know," said Leszek, "here at the university we always talked pretty freely among ourselves, but last year at this time not one of us would have dared to sit here with you. As for coming into the Bristol, picking you up in your room . . ." They looked at each other and roared. "Well, it would have meant three months in the clink," said Leszek.

"Six months," added Hania, the girl in the green woolen skirt.

"Well, those days are gone forever." They uttered a sigh of relief.

"Were you here last October—you know, that famous Friday?" I asked them.

They looked serious.

"Yes," answered Leszek, "all of us." With a sweeping gesture he pointed at the crowded cafeteria. "Everybody was here, thirty-two thousand of us. We did not go to bed for two days. We were ready to help Gomulka—and he knew it."

"Did you have arms?" I asked.

"No, but we knew where to get them. It was all pretty well laid out. Quite a weekend, that was!"

"And well worth it," chimed his companion. "Everything has been much, much better since then."

I looked at the boy's threadbare jacket and the girl's neatly darned blouse, at their lean, intelligent faces and the vitality that seemed to radiate out of them. They were poor; they had known the horrors of war in their childhood; they had never had any real security, even less the happy, carefree existence that youths in the world's happier countries consider as natural as the air.

Now, for the first time in their lives, they looked to the future with hope . . . because of the change since last October.

No matter to whom one talks in Poland, he will tell you that October was the milestone—it was the beginning of a new era and a beacon toward the future. The people who helped to make the revolution were the students, the writers, the newspaper and magazine editors backed by a solid mass of workers all over the country. On October 19, 1956, when Soviet tanks were surrounding the Warsaw Okecie Airport, when Russian divisions were converging on the Polish capital and Russian warships blocked all exits to the Baltic Sea, it was the young people and the workers who became the spokesmen for Poland and ranged themselves squarely behind Gomulka's brave stand.

The crisis had been brewing for six months. Khrushchev's

39121

Fernald Library
Colby Junior College
New London, New Hampshire

abrupt condemnation of Stalin in February and the people's
resentment at the dismal poverty they were living in slowly
brought to the surface the pressures building within the Polish
Communist Party. One section of Party leaders, called Stalinists or the Natolin group (named after a locality near Warsaw
where they used to meet), wanted to dig in against popular
pressure. "Never mind what the masses think, as long as we
control them," was their motto.

But the Party's majority, led by Edward Ochab, First Secretary of the Party, favored a more relaxed policy, consistent
with the people's desire for more freedom. Ochab, a tall man
in his fifties, with piercing blue eyes and unruly hair, played
a key role during October events. He had been "elected"
to his post only a few months before, following the death of
Moscow's faithful lieutenant, Boleslaw Bierut. Stalin had once
called Ochab "a real, tough Bolshevik with teeth that bite."

Khrushchev was convinced that here was a man whose devotion to Moscow could never be questioned. He made a
grave error of judgment. Ochab, an old battling Communist,
is also a man of undisputed honesty and a Polish patriot. It
did not take him long to become thoroughly outraged at the
constant stream of orders, counterorders and arrogant demands emanating from Moscow. Talking about his seven
months' tenure of office, he referred to it as "the most hor-
rible experience any man could be subjected to."

In the meantime it was becoming apparent that the Party
had lost control over the population and was becoming isolated. With the threat of economic collapse looming on the
horizon, the situation was rapidly getting out of hand. Something had to be done and soon.

The only remaining Communist of importance still popular in Poland was Wladyslaw Gomulka. He had been jailed
by Stalin five years before for opposing forced collectivization of farms and for refusing to denounce Tito. He was re-

leased from prison on Christmas Eve, 1954, though this was kept secret until April, 1956, when he was taken back into the fold of the Party—both as the best hope of the Stalinists and the white knight of the anti-Stalinist group. The Stalinists were to be sorely disappointed.

In May, Jacob Berman, the head of the Polish secret police, thought to be Moscow's No. 1 man in Poland, resigned as Deputy Premier. Next month the Poznan riots broke out. "No bread without freedom," chanted the Polish workers. Ochab bluntly declared that the government and the Party were to blame for the riots. When the trials of the Poznan rioters opened in September, they were held in the open and the sentences imposed were light.

Early in October, Hilary Minc, a Stalinist and Poland's economic czar, resigned from the Politburo. He had been accused of policies ruinous to Polish economy.

The Russians were becoming increasingly concerned. For some months now, significant changes had been taking place in the outlook of the Polish Communists. Many of them, while insisting they were still loyal to the Party, tended to look at Marxism as a historical and philosophical doctrine—one that needed to be substantially modernized to be still valid and applicable. Another change, even more noticeable, was their growing willingness to talk to non-Communist foreigners. They felt closer to them than to Russian or satellite fellow members who prattled the same dreary line almost word for word from yesterday's Party newspaper. A hurricane of thought was swirling through once-hermetic minds, and the gulf with Moscow was widening rapidly. As a result, the Polish press was becoming bitingly critical of the government and the Party. A large segment of it was openly anti-Russian.

Throughout most of September, Russian leaders shuttled between Warsaw and Moscow, trying to strengthen the influence of the Stalinists, who called themselves the "conservative" group. Gomulka was invited by Khrushchev for a conference and visit in the Crimea, supposedly as a cure for his ailing leg, the result of prison conditions.

"Thank you, comrade. Ciechocinek (a watering resort in Poland) will be sufficient," he replied.

While the pressures on First Secretary Ochab were mounting, he decidedly lined himself up with the "liberal wing" of the Party: Gomulka, Cyrankiewicz (the Prime Minister) and others. They nominated to important administrative posts people they trusted and who owed no allegience to Moscow. The Inner Security Police, under General Komar, a friend and prison colleague of Gomulka's, was organized to prevent a possible putsch. The workers were on their side. The Stalinists, on the other hand, were consolidating their ranks. Russian Marshal Rokossovsky, who was the commander-in-chief of the Polish Army, placed in key Army positions officers he trusted—mostly Moscow's stooges. General Witaszewski, a well-known Stalinist, was advanced to the rank of Deputy Commander-in-Chief.

Early in October, Poland was like a divided camp, with the liberals in the majority and the Stalinists an active and hostile minority. Against this background of tension, preparations were made for the projected meeting of the Central Committee of the Polish Communist Party which was to take place on Friday, October 19.

For ten days preceding the plenum, the Polish Politburo (the small governing body of the Central Committee) met each day with Gomulka, though he still held no official position in the Party. The Stalinists, realizing they had no hope of retaining control, tried to bargain for time and meanwhile strike a compromise with Gomulka. They found him intransigent.

"I have no desire to enter your Politburo," said the former prisoner. "The Politburo of which I become a member will be entirely reorganized and cleansed from top to bottom."

He also informed them that in no circumstances would he tolerate the presence in Poland of Rokossovsky. To this the Stalinists would not agree. They argued that Rokossovsky's dismissal from the Politburo would be a blow to his prestige in the Army and that the Russians would not allow it. Rokossovsky, a tall, bald, taciturn man, was heard to complain: "How can they exclude me from their Politburo, saying I have not been elected? I had *never* been elected to it. I was just *nominated* by Moscow."

But Gomulka stood firm. "You are afraid of the Russians?" he asked the Politburo members. "The main thing is not to be afraid of them. I have experienced their bullying tactics before. I remember when in 1944 Bulganin, then political commissar in Poland, arrived in Lublin and summoned me to appear forthwith. I sent the messenger back saying, 'If the Marshal is in a hurry, let him come to *my* house!' Imagine, a few minutes later he turned up, smiling, and we had a cordial discussion."

Ochab and Cyrankiewicz supported Gomulka. Their determination was strengthened by assurances received from Chinese leaders of China's "sympathetic backing for the 'Polish road to socialism.'" (Ochab received them when he traveled to China in September.)

In Moscow the situation was judged serious. An invitation was dispatched to Warsaw inviting all members of the Politburo, plus Gomulka, to come to the Russian capital for "immediate consultations." The invitation was declined.

The Russians wasted no time. About seven o'clock the morning of Friday, October 19, a Russian jet was sighted over Polish territory. It is five hours' flight between Moscow and Warsaw. The Soviet leaders, as is their custom, made their rapid decision and departed the Kremlin in the middle of the night. The news roused the Polish Politburo from their beds. Sleepy and irked at Russian insolence, they drove together with Gomulka to the military airport outside Warsaw which, though Polish, was run by the Russian Air Force. (One week later not one Russian was left there.) Out of the silvery Tupolev 104 walked a procession of Soviet Russia's ruling elite, headed by the short, squat, bull-necked and moon-faced First Secretary of the Russian Communist Party, Khrushchev. He was accompanied by Molotov, Mikoyan and Kaganovich, top members of the Soviet Presidium; Marshal Ivan Konev, commander of the Warsaw Pact forces; General Alexei Antonov, Chief of the Red Army General Staff, and other high-ranking military officials. It was quite an arrival.

Khrushchev's chunky body rolled down from the plane the minute the ramp was put into place. He turned to Rokossovsky, standing there in a full-dress uniform of the Commander of the Polish Army. They talked in Russian for a while.

According to an eyewitness account, Khrushchev became very angry at the news he heard from the General. "We shed our blood for Poland, and now they are trying to sell us out to the Americans!" he shouted. "But it won't work!"

Gomulka was standing nearby. He had never met Khrushchev. Now he thought that the bald little fat man was going too far. He called back: "We have shed more blood than you have, and we are not selling out to anyone."

This brought Khrushchev back with a start. He looked astonished at the stooping, quiet-voiced man in steel-rimmed glasses. He had no idea who that was. "*Kto ty tako?*" he demanded. ("Who are you?")

"I am Gomulka, whom you put in prison five years ago," came the answer.

Khrushchev stalked right past him and got into the car with Jozef Cyrankiewicz, the Polish Prime Minister, who greeted his unexpected guest with icy formality. The motorcade of Russian Zis, black Mercedes and Chevrolets carrying Polish officials sped toward the Belvedere Palace in Warsaw, a white stone mansion that used to be the home of Polish Presidents. There in the graceful Blue Room, furnished with French tea tables and satin upholstered chairs, formal discussions opened shortly before nine o'clock. It was to be a long day.

In the meantime, Warsaw was mobilizing.

"*They* are here," telephoned a member of the Warsaw Party organization to his wife, editor of a popular Polish weekly. Marta received the news calmly. The crisis was coming to a head. Her task had been outlined for some days; she knew exactly what to do. She sorted out her personal papers, straightened out her cluttered desk and telephoned her eight-year-old daughter, Nina, to say she would not be returning home that night. She got up and tidied her face at the mirror. She was an attractive small woman in her early thirties with curly blond hair and large, intelligent eyes. She put on her coat and walked down Nowy Swiat, headed for the Journalists' Club on Foksal Street. The time was a few minutes before noon. The day was cloudy and cold. The familiar street looked unchanged. Awareness of the Russian visit had not yet spread through the town. At the corner of Foksal Street late-season apples were being sold from a cart. Women were pressing around, wool scarves around their necks against the penetrating cold. Apples had been impossible to buy for some time. "I should buy some for Nina," thought Marta, the housewife taking over in her. "No, I won't," she decided. "Lord knows where I shall be tomorrow."

The trees had turned a deep red; the garden at the end of the street was full of mauve and pink asters. There was a sadness in the air, a hankering for the warm days that were gone.

The Polish Journalists' Club, a white stone and plaster, two-story classical building, was full of suppressed excitement. In the dining room overlooking the garden people were milling around exchanging the latest news. But few knew what was going on just several blocks down the street. A tall, bulky man with glasses came into the room hurriedly. He was Eligiusz Lasota, then editor of *Po Prostu,* the weekly of young Communist intellectuals, which for months had been in the forefront of the ferment toward liberalization. He too had heard the big news.

Viktor Woroszylski, editor of the *Nowa Kultura,* was there too. Thin, spruce and self-possessed, with a cool, inquisitive glance, he had been a Stalinist since his early teens. People used to remark that there was no more devoted child of the Kremlin than Viktor. A few years ago he and his wife went to Russia for a long visit. They studied at the Moscow University, traveled around the country, kept their eyes and ears open. They returned greatly changed. He was standing here now, hands in the pockets of his double-breasted gray suit, coolly discussing the situation.

They were all Communists. At least, they thought that they were, but in their minds Poland came first. They represented three of the most popular Polish weeklies which, together with the newspapers, had for months been waging a courageous campaign demanding that freedom of speech be restored, that dependence from Moscow be ended, that no more lies be told to the nation. They called themselves "the enraged." That was the way they felt about the state of their country.

They had the attentive ear of the nation. Now they were acting as intermediaries between the workers, the students, the restless Army officers and the Gomulka group on the Central Committee. Their object was to provide necessary backing for Gomulka, the leader they all trusted, because he had stood up to the Russians. Earlier in the week they had met secretly with delegations of workers from the Zeran Automobile Works in Warsaw, the largest factory in the city. They prepared pamphlets urging the Army to cooperate with them and sent emissaries throughout Poland to talk to soldiers and workers. A showdown was rapidly approaching. Arms were available, and they knew where to get them.

"I must get back to the office," said Lasota. They walked out into the street together. Marta drew her coat tight around her against the biting October wind.

"I am going to the Warsaw Committee," she said. "We shall probably have to wait until evening for orders."

The Warsaw Communist Party district committee was a pro-Gomulka group. Led by Stefan Staszewski, a handsome, intelligent man of great courage, it was to exert strong pressure on other Communist organizations throughout the country and help to swing them over to Gomulka.

In the old-fashioned gray building a round-the-clock headquarters had been organized by Staszewski. Couriers were dashing in and out, passing the word, "Be ready," to factories around Warsaw and to the 30,000-student body at the Warsaw University. Short-wave radio communications with other cities were being established, and dozens of additional telephone lines were hurriedly put in. It was now three o'clock. The Central Committee had met briefly that morning, formally re-elected Gomulka and three of his closest associates, then adjourned until the next day to allow its representatives to continue the talks with the Russians. The atmosphere was electric as reports about movements of troops were arriving. Warsaw was completely encircled by Russian troops advancing from the east and the west.

"Life is funny," thought Marta, perching on a crude, wooden stool next to a telephone that was to ring incessantly from now on. "How did it happen that I, a Communist, and others like myself, are here, prepared to fight the Russians with arms?"

She had been a Communist ever since she could remember. It was the Nazis' brutality against the Warsaw Jews that had convinced her, she thought, that the Communist doctrine meant justice. An ardent idealist, she had wanted a cause to work for. Most of her life had been lived inside Communism in the most immediate sense. Her husband was very close to the Central Committee; her friends were Communist intellectuals; the Party was her life. Now the Party was split; former theories were exploded. She was very confused but also exhilarated.

"This is the moment of truth," she thought suddenly, with elation. "We are going to sweep away all the lies; we shall build a new, decent Poland!"

The ring of a telephone cut into her thinking. It was Zeran, the automobile factory on the outskirts of Warsaw employing six thousand workmen. They wanted the Committee to know that they were now fully armed. The factory looked like a fortress; they were in touch with General Komar's militia troops, prepared to take to the streets at a moment's notice.

A teletype from Katowice in Polish industrial Silesia was brought in: "We miners, steelworkers and others of the Katowice, Sosnowiec and Bedzin workers' union are united and ready. Tell Gomulka we are all behind him."

"Lodz (Poland's second largest city) will stand with Gomulka," came a call from the town's Municipal Council.

"We have no arms," advised a textile mill at the outskirts of Lodz, "but our men are taking home bottles of sulphuric and hydrochloric acid, and all the knives we can find."

Zeran came on the line again. Workers' patrols, using the newly made factory cars, had gone out to meet a Polish division near Rembertow which had been ordered to move toward Warsaw.

"The soldiers are in an uproar!" shouted Gozdzik, the dynamic young foreman at Zeran. "The officers are with them. Not a shot will be fired unless it is at a Russian."

"Meetings have been going on since this morning. We are armed and will continue to keep watch," advised the Warsaw Polytechnic students.

The pile of messages was mounting. It was the same in other rooms on the floor. They were rapidly fed to couriers who sped with them to the Belvedere, where the fate of Poland hung in the balance. Gomulka's hand was being strengthened; he needed all the support he could muster. In spite of the Russians' promises earlier in the day that the movements of troops would be halted, news of their continuous progress streamed into the Belvedere Palace. The Poles had once threatened to break off negotiations. Now they were told that more troops were crossing into Poland from East Prussia. At Stettin a Russian force tried to cross the Oder River but withdrew when Polish soldiers fired at them.

There was dynamite in the smoke-filled air of the elegant French room with blue satin-covered chairs.

The talks focused on the key question: the Poles had announced their intention of liberalizing the regime, of finding "their own way to socialism." It would be "socialism with freedom," they explained to the Russians.

"You've got to stop it!" yelled Khrushchev. He was informed that the new Politburo would include Gomulka and that the Russian-imposed Rokossovsky had to go.

"Our people," said Gomulka, "date the Soviet occupation from the time of Rokossovsky's arrival. To us, he is the symbol of your domination. He has to go."

Khrushchev protested that this was impossible. "We shall resort to force, since there is no other way to convince you!"

he shouted, banging his fist and breaking the marquetry on a delicate 18th-century French table.

There were a few seconds of silence.

Slowly, as if rising with pain, Gomulka stood up. "Now it is my turn to say something," he declared in a slow, measured voice. "I don't want to make any more speeches in this room. I am going in front of the microphone right now and I will tell the Polish people what you demand of us and what we are refusing to grant you."

As the argument wore on the Russians perceived that the Poles would not budge. Everything bitter that could have been said was said that night. There was nothing left but to use force—or give in. With messages of support mounting behind Gomulka, it looked as if the whole nation was preparing to fight.

But the Poles wished to avoid violence. They sensed that members of the Russian Presidium were divided on how to cope with the situation, could be persuaded that Poland had no intention of becoming an anti-Russian state. Gomulka was shrewd enough to realize that under no circumstances could the Russian leaders give up their lines of communication with East Germany or allow Poland to pursue a foreign policy hostile to the Soviet Union. They could be pushed so far, and no farther.

Skillfully, to avoid provocation but without retreating an inch, Gomulka reviewed the extent of the economic collapse, the growing resentment at the political domination of Moscow and the spreading hatred of the Russians, the shameful economic exploitation, which he called "a grave Russian error," the failure of the Soviets to account for, let alone repatriate, some 500,000 Poles held by them since the first days of World War II. "There is no alternative," he argued. "Poland will either become a sovereign, independent state, still Communist and a good friend of the Russians, or you will have yourselves to blame for a nationwide uprising that will sweep Communism right from your very doorstep."

It was a delicately balanced speech and it achieved what it had set out to achieve. Gomulka and the rest of the Politburo agreed to come to Moscow in November to negotiate the economic issues and the future status of Soviet forces in Poland.

About 2 A.M. the negotiations finally drew to a close. The Russians were to leave at 3 A.M. They took off at 6:45.

In the meantime Warsaw was wide-awake. The Russian tanks had drawn a tight circle around the city, and several of them had ventured as far as the main thoroughfares. Driving with messages from the Warsaw Committee to the Belvedere Palace, Marta saw a large armored car ambling slowly down Aleje Ujazdowskie in the drizzle. The taxi driver pulled aside and got out. "Let's check whose it is," he said, "ours or *theirs*." It turned out to be General Waclaw Komar's militia. They went on.

The Belvedere Palace was surrounded by two opposing groups of security forces that glared furiously at each other. The Russians had brought with them, in their air fleet, droves of their own security people—as usual. Those surrounded the Belvedere on all sides. The Poles, not to be outdone and afraid for the security of their leaders, drew a cordon around the Russian police. It was hard to tell who was guarding whom at the moment. Groups of students stood outside the gates of the garden; the streets were full of people, as in daylight. Everybody was silent and watchful.

Marta delivered a pile of teletyped messages to a Polish militiaman at a side entrance and stood outside for a while talking to a group of students. A small man in a dark-beige raincoat came up to her silently. "I have been trying to reach you all evening," he said. "Please do not sleep at home tonight. It is better." He went off and was lost in the night.

Marta had been expecting the warning. One by one, all of

Warsaw's newspaper editors had been quietly told by the security police that they were in danger of being arrested. "Stay away from home, if you can," anonymous telephone calls warned them.

It was later disclosed that pro-Soviet officers of the Natolin group had drawn up a list of about seven hundred principal supporters of Gomulka in the government, the Party, among the workers and leading intellectuals in the city, and planned to arrest them during the night. It was a secret plan for a putsch that was to swing the country over to the control of the Natolin group. But the secret police—until now a dreaded and sinister force—refused to act on their orders. Together with volunteers from among the workers of Zeran, they stood quiet guard over the buildings where the seven hundred lived.

"Times are changing," chuckled one of the students. "I never would have believed the *Bezpieka* (secret police) would range itself on *our* side!"

Back at the Committee headquarters, excitement was at a fever pitch. Messages were being relayed from Polish Army detachments holding all-night meetings throughout the country. They planned to arrest Russian officers in their midst. Polish Air Force units at Deblin put armed guards around the hangars with orders to shoot "if the Russians use force." Naval units at sea radioed that they were steaming back to home ports. With Russian warships blocking the exits to the Baltic, the danger of a clash was apparent. Over six thousand factories declared their readiness to stand by Gomulka.

But the most explosive spot in the nation was Warsaw. Uprisings were nothing new to this city. That night, as it stayed wide-awake, with thousands of workers armed and militia patrolling the streets, ready to pounce on a Russian soldier or tank, violence was just under the surface. It only needed an incident to flame out.

Stefan Staszewski stood leaning against the porcelain stove, absently stirring the sugar in a glass of hot tea. His face was ashen-gray with fatigue. "Something has to be done about Warsaw—the tension in the city is too great," he said. "We must find out exactly what goes on."

He asked Marta to go to Gomulka and bring back direct orders what to do.

It was now 4 A.M., Saturday, October 20.

Gomulka lived in an old two-story house in Saska Kepa, in the Warsaw suburb of Praga, where he and his wife Zofia occupied a three-room apartment and kitchen. There was a small garden in front and an old warehouse opposite. No police detail had been assigned to guard him, but the house was surrounded by students who on their own accord decided that "he should be protected." The door was wide-open, and the entrance was crowded with people.

Gomulka stood in the narrow, beige-papered hallway—a frail, lean, stooping figure in the grayish light of the dawn. "He is still wearing that old gabardine suit," thought Marta, noticing the light, loose-fitting jacket, the outsize pockets and the sleeves about an inch and a half too long. She remembered it from the days of the war. This was the only good suit he owned then—this and two pairs of work trousers. His face remained in the shadow, but his voice was precise and betrayed no fatigue.

"Warsaw may go back to sleep and relax," he said briefly, when Marta gave him the report. "It's all right for the moment. *They* are leaving."

She drove back with the orders, a sense of elation rising within her. It was now light outside: a new day was beginning. In front of the newly built sports stadium people were waiting to board a red-painted trolley bus. A pale, shy autumn sun warmed the Vistula waters. The little boats on the river were chugging along as usual. At the corner where

the wide Aleje Jerozolimskie crosses the narrow arc of
Nowy Swiat a cavalcade of black cars flanked by outriders
passed her at breakneck speed. They turned left toward the
airport.

Marta stopped and got out of the car, next to a vegetable
stand run by an old peasant woman bundled up in a sweater
and a black kerchief tied under her chin. "There they go;
they have left. They did not even stop to have breakfast,"
mused the old woman, opening the shop for the day's business.

The good news spread through the city rapidly. In the
offices of the *Po Prostu* on Wiejska Street, a small, inconspicuous old house across the street from the white classical
building of the Polish Parliament, the young, firm, youthful
faces of the staff wore masks of heavy fatigue.

"I shall never forget this night," said Lasota. He wiped his
forehead and took off his glasses, bleary-eyed.

"Go to bed. We have won, the Russians are leaving," he
signaled to coöperative No. 177 which, like hundreds of
others in the past twenty-four hours, was affirming its readiness to stand by.

Thus ended a tense forty-eight hours' vigil.

Next day the people went wild, as if drunk with the newly
acquired freedom.

Although the Russian troops were still poised within shoot-
ing distance from the city, cheering crowds filled the streets.
There was a tremendous demand for papers. Warsaw newspapers printed extra editions every few hours, and taxi drivers
volunteered to deliver them to the streets free of pay. At the
Journalists' Club in Foksal Street a banquet was held by the
Warsaw Newspapermen's Association. Late that afternoon,
in a speech to the Central Committee, Wladyslaw Gomulka,
whom people affectionately began to call "Wieslaw," pre-

sented the nation with a virtual declaration of independence from the Soviet Union:

"Poland has the right to be sovereign, and this sovereignty must be respected.

"The agricultural policy of the past (Soviet-directed) has brought ruin to individual farmers. Inefficient collectives will be disbanded.

"The only way to raise our standard of living is to produce more, cheaper and better. . . .

"Sweeping the country in the most powerful wave is a desire for democratization of our way of life, for freer exchange of thought, for liquidation of the hated remnants of a rigid and inefficient system imposed upon us from outside. This democratization will continue relentlessly. . . .

"The roads to socialism may be various. We are no doctrinaires. There is the Soviet way; there is the Yugoslav way; there is also another way. . . ."

On Sunday, October 21, a lovely autumn day, long lines formed everywhere in front of newspaper kiosks, waiting to buy the full text of that historic speech. The entire nation rallied behind Gomulka's leadership. "The Army is with the people; the people are with the Army in defense of democratization," proclaimed banners over the Warsaw University buildings. Most of the students knew little about the details of the negotiations. It was enough for them that the long-demanded change of leadership had taken place within the Party and that Rokossovsky was about to leave Poland.

Three days later the whole of Warsaw attended a huge rally where the new First Secretary of the Polish Workers Party spoke to a wildly cheering crowd. Shops closed; cafes were deserted; tram service was infrequent—even street stands were deserted. All over town scribbled notices appeared pasted over the doors: "Gone to the meeting. Will return when it's over."

Not only Warsaw, but the entire nation was stirring. A
new era had dawned. For the first time in seventeen years
there was hope in the unhappy and devastated land. Like a
great powerful wind, Gomulka's words swept over the 120,-
ooo square miles of Poland. From the gray shores of the Baltic
to the snowy peaks of the Tatras one word was being heard:
Change.

And things began to change fast. Out of ten thousand collectives more than 8700 were disbanded. Some fell apart overnight; some waited for the crops to come in. The powerful
UB, Poland's secret police employing thousands of agents,
suddenly ceased to exist. The cumbersome Party apparatus
parallel to the State administration was cut down to the bone,
and local officials found themselves on their own once again.
In a move of joyous spontaneity Army units throughout the
land cleansed themselves of their Russian advisers and sent
them packing. Newspapers and magazines came out free and
uncensored, and everywhere people began to talk and say
whatever was on their minds. Practically overnight, without
a drop of blood being shed, the largest and the most powerful Russian satellite, the pivot of the Warsaw Pact, with 28
million people and 22 crack Army divisions, slid away from
the Russian embrace and began to move slowly on the road
toward independence. The nation's rush to freedom was so
powerful that it seemed nothing could stop it in its course.

But during the fortnight that followed, Poland watched
with horror as Soviet tanks and troops shot down thousands
of Hungarian men and women who were fighting for the
very things they wanted. It was a shattering warning, and
throughout the country elation gave way to a sense of grim
reality. The people now realized what their government had
known for some time: that to the Kremlin the loss of direct
control over Poland was a bitter setback. In the blazing light
of Budapest they saw that they could push the colossus so

far, but no farther. The Kremlin might permit a Communist regime to be non-Soviet, but it would not permit any regime to be anti-Communist. The dreams of a truly independent Poland had to be set aside for the moment.

From the beginning of the Hungarian uprising there was intense sympathy for the insurgents. Poland and Hungary had always been close. One of the greatest Polish kings was a Hungarian, Stefan Batory, Prince of Transylvania (1576-1586). During the thousand-year history of their existence the two nations had never fought. "The Poles and the Hungarians are like brothers," said an old Polish proverb coined in the 16th century.

Now thousands of people hurried to give blood and to send medical supplies to the Hungarians. Hundreds of students, writers and workers, many of them Communist Party members, crossed the frontier illegally into Hungary to fight in Budapest on the side of the insurgents. "We showed them how to build barricades; we had more practice than they've had," said a prominent Polish writer when I talked to him three months later.

Trybuna Ludu, the official Polish Communist Party organ, appealed to the Soviets angrily to "stop spilling the blood of our brothers, the Hungarians." The Soviet theory about Western agents being responsible for the uprising was dismissed with contempt. At the United Nations the Polish delegate, for the first time since 1945, failed to vote with the Soviet Union.

After the uprising was crushed, a great sadness came over Poland. There was revulsion at the Soviet atrocities in Budapest, but also an immense relief that the country had been spared the Hungarian blood bath. The people took stock of the gains that their own "quiet revolution" had brought them and turned to Communist Gomulka in the hope that he could steer a middle course.

"He has proved that he can stand up to the Russians and that while he cares for Communism he cares far more for Poland," was the frequently expressed view. It was on this basis that they voted overwhelmingly for him in the crucial January elections, two months later.

"You do not think that he will let you down and slide back, do you?" I asked Marta last March while walking down Nowy Swiat. We had stopped to read a headline announcing a change-over in the editorial staff of the *Trybuna Ludu.* Only six months had elapsed since October, but censorship was coming back to the press. "Wieslaw," the hero of the intellectuals, was tightening the screw on his admirers.

She shook her curly hair violently. "There will never be any going back to the pre-October days. This is impossible," she said. "We may not yet be able to print the whole truth, but we shall *never* again be compelled to print lies. Wieslaw has economic reasons for doing it. The Russians are sensitive to what they read in our press, and this in turn has bearing on deliveries of crucial raw materials. Things will get better after the American loan is received."

Two months later, one of Marta's best friends was dismissed from her post as deputy editor of the popular Polish weekly, *Swiat.* She had written an article entitled "To the Comrades of the Fraternal Parties," addressed to Communist parties in East Germany, Czechoslovakia, Rumania and Bulgaria, in which she accused them of deliberately misrepresenting the events of the Polish October. She said that all Communists should begin to ask themselves the question "whether we want only to preserve power or to preserve socialism." She was immediately attacked by *Neues Deutchland*, the chief Communist paper of East Germany, who called her a "renegade seeking to liquidate Communism." *Kommunist*, the Soviet Party's ideological monthly, took up the attack with a fury. The incident happened at a time when Poland was particularly dependent on Russia for supplies. The negotiations in Washington had been dragging on for four months; their outcome was uncertain. Though the dismissal was made the subject of a special resolution by the Secretariat of the Polish Communist Party, Marta's friend was quietly allowed to continue working in journalism, but not to hold a responsible position at the moment. Lucrative full-time translation jobs were quietly pushed her way.

Marta took the news calmly. Her faith in Wieslaw never wavered. "He *had* to do it," she told me. "It's all right. He still will look after her. I shall see him in a few months, and we shall both discuss it freely. A year ago she would have been in prison, but not now. She is safe. That's what October has brought."

I remembered the words I had heard spoken at random during the first weeks after my arrival in Poland.

"What change did October bring to you and to your family's life?" I asked Zenon Poninski, a small, blue-eyed man, with a cheerful face and a lock of grayish-blond hair. He was a road engineer in Lowicz, a town forty miles west of Warsaw. He, his wife and three children lived in a one-and-a-half-room apartment with no running water and no bath. Two other families shared their kitchen. He earned 3000 zlotys a month, about $125, barely enough to feed a family of five. There never was enough money for clothes.

"There has been no immediate change in my standard of living—or at least not as yet," he said laughing. "That modern two-room apartment with our own bath and a kitchen still looks like the faraway dream that it is. But mentally everything is *quite* different. This is Poland again; there is not the slightest doubt about it. We can talk, laugh and grumble; we write whatever we please. If I want to apply for a job, I don't need to be investigated by the secret police any more. My wife has relatives in Toronto, and she now mails her letters from the corner mailbox, instead of having to register them at the General Post Office downtown. And we get mail much faster, since Gomulka fired all the censors."

We walked down the wide cobblestone street to the station. The road was lined with makeshift kiosks selling everything from vegetables to shoes and infant wear. Women were crowding around, their clothes shabby but clean. "All this has cropped up since October," my friend pointed out with a smile. "Where they get their wares from, nobody knows, but they are better and nicer looking than in the State-owned shops. The whole town has livened up since. We have two new restaurants, four shoe stores, three dress shops, a blacksmith, a hairdresser and a cabinetmaker; new grocery and vegetable stores are opening up each week. Housewives here do not have to line up for meat any longer. Why go to the State store when the private butcher gives you better meat anyway? Since private farmers around here were given a chance to earn a decent living, the supplies to the town have trebled."

We came to the railroad station. "You see the big man standing there," my friend said pointing to a towering individual in a brown leather jacket. "He used to be in UB— now he is unemployed. His wife had to go to work last October, so he had to line up for the coal. One morning he was pelted with eggs by women who for years had been storing grudges against him. Still, he has to stay here. With the terrible shortage of rooms, there is no other bed in the country for him to sleep in."

October did bring a change to all Poles. The sinister, all-embracing Party apparatus had suddenly receded into the background. The omnipresent and omniscient State, the all-controlling and all-directing giant acting in the name of vast anonymous masses, has relinquished its hold on its victims and left them free to shape their own destinies.

"In the old days we had to review the accounts of all businesses around here," said the local official in Siedlce, a town halfway between Warsaw and the Russian border. "All questions had to be referred in detail to the Ministry of Commerce in Warsaw. It took weeks for a decision to come through. Now we don't care what they do, and they seem to be far better off for it."

He looked around the large, spacious room and the three telephones on his desk. "This telephone used to ring constantly," he said. "Orders and counterorders streamed down from Party headquarters in Warsaw. They never came to see us. The closest Party officials ever got to the people was on the telephone. That's why they had so many of them on their desks. It gets a little lonely here sometimes, and one is not used to taking responsibility. But people seem to like it better this way," he added with a broad, philosophical smile.

A week later I was in Stettin, Poland's westernmost port on the Baltic. The town was bursting with activity. A canning factory, a vegetable-processing plant and a tannery had all been opened since Christmas. People were cleaning rubble from the streets. "We never cared about it until lately," said a husky young resident hard at work with a wheelbarrow and a shovel.

Along the tree-lined boulevard circling the approach to the sea a cement wall was being dismantled.

"The town is taking over the port area," explained an inhabitant. "Before, nobody was allowed near the water—security reasons, you know. The best part of our town was thus closed to the people. Why should our port be run by bureaucrats in Warsaw? It made no sense—but then, it's only now that things are beginning to make sense."

So spoke the people in Poland when I arrived there in the

winter of 1957. The entire country was stirring and getting busy. There was hope—but over the newly won freedom loomed the threat of an economic catastrophe.

Twelve years of Stalinist rule have ruined a once-prosperous country. Poland used to be known as one of Europe's chief granaries; but today, after years of senseless farm exploitation and forcible collectivization, it is unable to feed its own people. Its industry, built according to a master plan conceived and developed in Moscow, without regard to local Polish conditions or needs of the population, ran on huge subsidies and was fantastically mismanaged by a vast army of "experts" whose only qualification for jobs was the right shade of political opinion. As a result, the workers, who were to be the first beneficiaries of the socialist paradise, have today a far lesser purchasing power than they had before the war.

"We all love and support Gomulka," a Warsaw factory worker said to me. "He is an honest man and a good Pole. But we have to earn more money; otherwise, the freedom we gained last October will turn out to be meaningless."

This worker was making what in Poland is called a good salary. He earned 2500 zlotys a month—roughly $100. The rent on his apartment was low; but with inferior-quality meat costing eighty cents a pound, butter at over a dollar, sugar at $1.35, staples in short supply and expensive, it was hardly enough to feed his family of four. He owned one suit of clothes and a pair of worn-out dungarees. A new pair of shoes of poor-quality leather cost around 700 zlotys—one third of his monthly earnings. And if, after months of saving, coupled with intricate black-market operations, he managed to get enough money to buy some of the acutely needed essentials, the shoddy quality of the goods made all his efforts frustrating.

"The consumer be damned!" was the unspoken principle

of the pre-October regime. The Russians, while forcing Poland to create a top-heavy economy designed to serve Soviet interests by concentrating on heavy industry and armaments, put all the emphasis on quantity of production. The quality did not matter. No wonder that, with few and poor-quality consumer goods to reward people for hard work, production in mines, shops and farms slumped to a desperate level!

How to raise the standard of living and create enough incentive to make people work harder is the first and foremost objective of Gomulka's government. Nobody, except a few in the inner councils of the Party, knows the full extent of the economic debacle. A team of nonpolitical experts has been given the task of breaking down the rigid State controls and forging more elastic economic policies.

The future of Poland will depend on how well they succeed and how quickly.

CHAPTER 4

A Coffee=House Interview

JERZY PUTRAMENT was the first Polish Communist of importance that I met. Member of Parliament, well-known political writer, friend and supporter of Gomulka, he had played an important part during the crucial days of the October change-over. His critics liked to point out that his past had been somewhat "murky"; he changed skins like a lizard, they said. But it was generally conceded that he had a good mind, agile and trained for years to skip through a maze of Communist theory with assurance. In the constantly shifting political patterns of the Party, this mastery had been his chief asset; it had won him the high position that he occupied today. He liked to think of himself as an intellectual. His background among Polish Communists was unusual: he came from an old family of Lithuanian nobility and became a Communist while a student at the University of Wilno, as a protest against Hitler's inhuman program, he once said. He went to Russia in 1941 and returned to Poland in the summer of 1945 with the victorious Red Army. He had been in the news ever since.

My friend Roman had met him in Paris, when Putrament was Polish Ambassador to France in the early postwar years; he then was a Stalinist. In October, 1956 he was for Gomulka.

59

He even was for the Church and urged in his writing that freedom of religion be restored. The following spring, however, he was again arguing the Stalinist position in two articles he wrote for a Polish weekly.

Roman arranged that the three of us meet for tea at the Switezianka café near the Bristol. Switez is the name of a lake near the Lithuanian town of Wilno—the theme of a romantic ballad by Mickiewicz. Putrament came from Wilno.

One of the reasons for my interest in him was the very particular affinity and love I had always felt for the countryside around Wilno, which in my day used to belong to Poland. Now it is a part of the Baltic provinces, incorporated with Russia. Its people have been deported and killed off.

It was a land of lakes, clear rivers, pine forests and gentle hills—a remote geographical area tucked away at the edge of the Western world between the Baltic Sea and the Russian border. The people who lived there were Lithuanian, but they had been part of Poland since the 14th century, when the pagan Lithuanian Prince Jagiello married the saintly Polish Queen Jadwiga and brought the whole of Lithuania into the Commonwealth of Poland and the embrace of the Roman Catholic Church.

They grew rye, potatoes and flax, worked in the forests and made elaborate wood carvings in the winter. Their agricultural methods went back to the last century. The countryside around Wilno was still virgin. There were few roads; electricity was unknown. Horse carriages, bicycles, canoes and an occasional train ride were the only means of communication in existence. The myriads of islands on the lakes to which, as children, we used to row in canoes were covered with tall, luscious grass; ribbons of white mists from the hills danced around them in the sun. We thought that no human being had tread on them before us. Nowhere else in the country did the nightingales sing so sweetly; nowhere else did the jasmin grow into such huge, towering trees. The country was rich with folk legends and old-fashioned, half-pagan rituals. I remember a midsummer night one year, at the house of an uncle near Wilno—a rambling one-story manor with white pillars overgrown with glycinias—when with assorted cousins and playmates we set off to find the blooming flower of the fern.

"This is the one night in the year when the fern blooms," said the old, local legend, which went back to the days of the pagans. "If you can see the flower of the fern at midsummer, you will always be happy in your life."

We tramped for hours in the woods, bathed in the soft moonlight, as in magic; we lay on thick carpets of moss, listened to the croaking of the frogs and recited Lithuanian ballads aloud. We were intensely happy. I still think of it with delight. Nature in that part of the world was benign: no snakes, no poison ivy lurked in ambush; there were few mosquitoes and few flies. In summer the nightingale filled the woods.

On Saint John's Day, which came on the twenty-fourth of June, the lakes and the streams were alight with floating wreaths—the wreaths of Saint John, they were called. We made them out of long-stemmed flowers and of reeds and let them float down with the current. At night, wood fires were built along the banks of the water, and young people danced around them singing folksongs. No one could tell the origins of the custom; it must have come down from the ancient Slavs.

Wilno lies in a deep, rounded valley, surrounded by hills on all sides. People called it the "woodland capital," because dark pine forests closed in on it from all sides. The beginnings of the town went back to the 10th century. Legend had it that a Lithuanian chieftain fell asleep by the fire after a strenuous day's hunting. He dreamed that the four-faced god

Swiatowid appeared before him and asked that a town be
built on the very spot where he stood. I remember it mostly
as a city of churches—there were so many of them in the
town—white, with gleaming gold and red towers, built by
Italian architects in the opulent baroque style. They were the
most distant outposts of Western architecture in Europe.
There was an ancient university in Wilno, an important
center of Catholic and Jewish studies; a miraculous picture
of Our Lady was built into a doorway at the end of a long,
narrow street. I liked the twisting streets of the town, filled
with peasants fresh from the countryside in their horsecarts;
the street stands, where one could buy pretzel-like little rolls
and wood carvings; the bustle and laughter of the market.

I did not know Mr. Putrament in those days, but we must
have passed each other without knowing and rubbed shoulders in the constantly crowded streets.

"How old is he now?" I asked Roman, as we were nearing the Switezianka café. "He must be in his late forties. He
was a student at Wilno in the thirties. You will find him a
good conversationalist, he loves to talk."

All I saw of him first were his legs—very long, with large
feet, stretched straight in front of him at the table. The rest
was hidden from view by a widely spread newspaper
mounted on a long, wooden stick. He was engrossed in his
reading and did not see us approaching. He had a well-shaped
longish face, graying hair, a straight nose, blue-gray eyes,
large, square, but well-manicured hands. He got up and
greeted us with the easy assurance of a man of the world.
I did not like his voice; it had a hard, metallic sound which
put one on guard, but I forgot about it as we talked.

I sat next to him on the sofa. He pointed to a headline in
the evening paper on the table: "Senator Knowland says . . .
if the Poles need bread, let Russia give it to them." A wire-
service dispatch, quoting Senator Knowland's speech in Chi-

cago objecting to the proposed Polish loan, was spread across the front page in thick type.

I had heard the news earlier; the foreign correspondents at the Bristol had got it in telegrams from their papers. Roman and I had talked about it on our way from the Bristol. To me, Senator Knowland's attitude was rigid and inhuman. It seemed like a short-sighted policy to treat the satellite bloc as an unchangeable monolith. The Poles had shown great courage in standing up to the Russians; they had always leaned to the West and expected us to help them. They should not be pushed back into the Russian embrace only because they have to get bread from somewhere. They did not want Russian help; they had just liberated themselves—at least, to a certain extent. I dreaded to think of the disappointment and widespread feeling of letdown that this pronouncement would cause in the country. I doubted that I would be able to face the Warsaw University students the next day. They had looked to the United States with such hope.

I remarked to Mr. Putrament that Senator Knowland represented only one segment of the American public and that his opinion did not mean our going back on the promises we made to Poland in October.

He replied: "Still, it is going to be rough sliding for Kotlicki (the head of the Economic Delegation) in Washington. The longer the negotiations, the less psychological impact your aid is going to have here. I told them not to expect too much: I know the West; they have no understanding of our problems."

Last October Mr. Putrament was so enthusiastic in Gomulka's support that *Pravda* rebuked him for saying that he preferred "imperialist Coca-Cola to the best home-distilled vodka."

"You know," he said, puffing on a Chinese cigarette in a holder, "Poland's relationship to the West strikes me as a case of unrequited love: the aftermath of unrequited love is usually bitterness and sarcasm. But people here will not admit it as yet."

He turned to Roman. "What they all fail to grasp in the West is that the world is now irrevocably divided in two halves—the Red and the non-Red. Because of our geographical position, we shall have to remain on the Red side of the globe. We can't help it: we have to live here. But—and this is very important—Poland's Communism has evolved into something that is humane, flexible and easy to live with; something new is being molded here. We do not know ourselves yet what it is. If this experiment in freedom is allowed to last, it will have a most tremendous impact on the remaining Red half of the globe. It will unloosen forces that until now have been rigidly held in check; it will bring our Red half closer to the West and make understanding possible. It would seem obvious that the United States should encourage us in paving the way to a gradual humanization of the Communist system."

He stopped to pour me some tea, then swung his large body over in my direction. "All this is self-evident, but your people do not see it this way. They would like us to adopt the capitalistic system in full. First of all, the Russians would walk in if we did. But, what is more important, our people do not want it. They are afraid they would be exploited again, as they were in the days of feudal landlords and industrial cartels. This country has never been a democracy in the real sense of the word. Our most important task at the moment is to improve the standard of living. Limited private initiative is good; the worker will be happier and work better, but State planning has to be the basis of any socialist economy, including our own."

We talked for a while about Wilno and the countryside we both knew.

"When did you become a Communist," I asked him, "and why?"

He answered: "It happened in the early thirties. I witnessed too many nationalist excesses at the university; too many Jewish students were beaten by my colleagues. Communism seemed like a more humane creed than Hitler's slogans pouring out of our radios."

This, of course, was not exactly the truth. Before he became a Communist, Putrament had gone through a period of violent Nazi-like nationalism. He was one of the most rabid anti-Semites in Wilno. Then he swung right around to Communism. It must have been quite a difficult decision to make, to become a Communist in those days. Poland had been a Russian province for over a hundred years. Its independence was relatively recent and cherished by all. If Communism was to win, the country would become a Russian province again. The Communist Party was illegal. Comparatively few people joined it; suspected members were hunted down and jailed. Wilno was about 87 miles from the Russian border, but that border was hermetically closed. Putrament's family and traditions must have been an obstacle, but he disregarded everything, went ahead and joined the Party. Power was what he wanted: he was going to get it—for a price.

When, in September 1939, the German armies poured into Poland, the Russians met them halfway. They occupied the eastern part of the country and started deporting civilians on a mass scale. Men, women and children were inhumanly packed into crude cattle cars, taken East to slavery in Siberian coal mines or the frozen wastes of Kazakstan. Among the deportees were both of Putrament's parents and his two younger sisters. His father died in forced labor, but his son's loyalty to the Soviets was not affected by his death. Putrament became one of the first members of the Committee of Liberation, the nucleus of the puppet government the Rus-

sians were going to impose on the Poles. Together with the
Russian armies, halted on the Vistula River, he watched the
agonizing fight of the Polish Home Army in Warsaw without lifting a finger to help them. The Home Army represented the London government in exile. Putrament had sided
with the Russians. He was being coldly logical. But something
must have happened to him there and then. As with many
diehard Polish Communists, the ruthlessness of the Russians
was beginning to sow germs of resentment. The years he
spent as Polish Ambassador to France opened his eyes to the
many pleasant sides of the West. Now he wanted the best of
the two systems; he obviously was not going to stick his neck
out in either direction. He was an old professional at the game.

We talked about freedom of the press for awhile. He felt
that many of the young newspaper editors—"the hotheads,"
he called them—who were in the forefront of Gomulka's national movement, were "going too far. They carry on as if
Poland were about to become a Western-style democracy—
and as if it were located in Patagonia. They forget that the
Russians are barely a hundred miles away, watching every
move that we make."

When I mentioned a prominent pro-Gomulka Polish newspaperman, Putrament shrugged his shoulders in disgust. "He
is no better than the others—no judgment, no common sense
—just drunk with the newly acquired freedom. The Party is
split; the country is drifting into anarchy, and Gomulka is
reluctant to curtail the press. It will all end badly."

Soon after our conversation several of the most vocal
young editors were dismissed or quietly told to conform. The
rest were bitterly disappointed, but as one of them said, "I
cannot fight Wieslaw on this; he must have his reasons for
doing it."

We went out into the street. Roman was hurrying to the
theater to see a new Polish play, *Aszantka*, an excellent con-

temporary drama, as I was to see a week later. Mr. Putrament suggested he would give me a lift to the Bristol. He waved a thick walking cane at a passing taxi, looking for all the world like a typical Lithuanian country squire exhorting his peasants to work. The same thought must have occurred to Roman, because we looked at each other and smiled.

We slowed in front of the Church of St. Saviour, from which crowds were pouring out after vespers. "Are you an atheist?" I asked my silent companion in the taxi.

"But of course," he said, smiling with indulgence, indicating that only a woman could ask him such a preposterous question.

"I hear that thousands of Polish Communists go to church; some get married under the cover of night," I went on. "How do you explain this phenomenon?"

"Well, it's all in the old Polish tradition," he said softly. "The people just won't give up. Also"—and he roared with laughter as the taxi came to a halt—"they are probably afraid of their wives!"

I said good-bye and thanked him for giving me so much time in a week when the Parliament was in session.

"You are easier to look at than most of my Central Committee colleagues," he responded, bowing gallantly. "I'll see you at the Sejm (Parliament). Good-bye."

I watched him walk in the direction of the Old City Square, swinging his cane as he went.

When I told my Aunt Zofia that I had tea with Putrament, she was shocked. "How could you!" she exclaimed. "Don't you know that he is an atheist and a man who should never be trusted? Why, he may even let our Gomulka down one day, he has changed allegiance so often!"

I pointed out that *our* Gomulka was also an atheist and

that she had trusted him enough to give him her vote last January.

"Oh, that's quite different!" retorted my conservative aunt, the pillar of the neighborhood churches. "Gomulka is a good Pole. We need him; he is the only one we have at the moment."

She reflected the feelings of most Poles.

CHAPTER 5

Gomulka at First-Hand

THE new Parliament (the Sejm), elected in January, was to convene at 4 P.M. Poles all over the country had been looking forward to it eagerly. The Assembly was of course expected to be dominated by Gomulka's United Workers' Party (Communist), but the composition of the new Sejm was vastly different from that of its predecessor. The United Peasants, the Democratic and the Independent parties, all of them non-Communist, took up 49 percent of the seats; among the Independents there were twelve Roman Catholic deputies.

"Our Sejm will no longer remain mute," said Boleslaw Drobner, a Communist deputy, opening the new Parliament. "It will not be a parliamentary fiction, as it has been in the past. It must and shall be a furnace in which we will be forging iron and steel as long as our October remains hot."

The concept of a freely debating parliamentary body forging the laws in a Communist-dominated country was just one more of the paradoxes of the "strange Polish situation," but nobody, including Mr. Gomulka, seemed to find it unusual. It was part of the "Polish way to socialism" and of the process of the gradual humanization of the "Red half of the globe" that Mr. Putrament had been talking about.

The day was sunny and cold. Long lines of people stood in

front of the white-colonnaded building of the Sejm, waiting to obtain admission to the public gallery. Interest in the opening was intense.

Sydney Gruson of the New York *Times* and his wife Flora were talking together in the white marble rotunda next to the press gallery entrance. Behind them gardeners were putting finishing touches to a bank of crimson geraniums and mauve potted hydrangeas. Dark-haired and slender, dressed in well-cut classic suits, Flora is a top political reporter in her own right. With her slow, precise voice and mercilessly logical mind, she is a match for the best-trained Communist dialecticians. "This woman thinks like a man," Warsaw intellectuals referred to her with respect. Sydney's warm, affectionate nature, great personal charm and outstanding professional ability made him the best-informed and most-popular foreign newspaperman in Warsaw. "Gruson knows everything," a high-ranking Polish official exclaimed in mock despair, when a detailed account of Gomulka's top-secret trip to Moscow last May appeared on the front page of the New York *Times*.

"I hear the Catholic deputies have founded a club called 'the Cardinals,' " said Flora. "It's nice. The Independents will now start one called the '19th of October'—I'd like to know what the PPR's (Communist) is going to be." She strolled down the hall, followed by admiring glances of newly-elected parliamentarians.

I went into the press gallery and looked at the gathering below. The Communist deputies, who with 237 members have 51.7 percent of the seats, took up the left half of the hall. The Peasants and the Democrats sat in the center; the Independents, including the Catholics, were on the right.

In the front row of the benches sat Gomulka. His presence towered over the vast semicircular chamber. Every speech on the floor had mentioned his name—he himself did not speak.

Thousands of eyes were on him, but he pensively gazed away in the distance—detached and solitary in spite of the rays of affection that seemed to flow toward him from the deputies' benches on the floor, from the closely packed galleries of spectators and from the crowds gathered outside the Parliament building, eager to get a glimpse of him from the distance. Here he was—a calm, reserved, prematurely aged man, the Communist leader of a fiercely anti-Communist nation, the man of whom even the most ardent Polish patriots spoke affectionately as *"swoj"* ("our own")—the highest compliment a people with a hard history could bestow on a politician. *"Swoj"* implies confidence, and Gomulka has it. It is a tentative confidence, one he may lose if he fails to keep faith, but the longer he justifies it, the more it will grow into love. The Poles say of Gomulka, "He is our own." They also say, "He is wise." By steering a middle course in a political situation fraught with danger and unparalleled complexity, he won the gratitude of the people and their trust. "He knows what he is doing," they reason. They are grateful for the change he already has brought to their lives; and though their longing for freedom is intense, most comply when he bluntly tells them to be patient. They like his modesty and simple, almost austere way of life. There are no busts of Gomulka anywhere in the country; his photographs are few and rarely seen.

How did this diehard Communist earn such a harvest of faith? There was nothing about the first forty years of his life to indicate that he would someday become the national hero of the Poles, the majority of whom abhor the basic ideas to which he had devoted his life. In prewar days he was known as one of the most fanatical and ruthless Communists; his activities were illegal and he was haunted by the police. Under the name of "Comrade Duniak" he spread Communist propaganda, infiltrated trade-unions and spent most of his time in jail for anti-State agitation. Son of a poor oil worker in Krosno, in southern Poland, he started to work as a plumber at fourteen and joined the ranks of the revolutionaries at an early age. He was idealistic and physically very brave. "A tough and obstinate spirit," his colleagues said of him. Once, during one of his recurrent sojourns in prison, he shared a cell with six other Communists; disagreeing with their interpretation of some of Marx' ideological points, he refrained from speaking to them for eighteen months. He was in jail again in 1938, when Stalin ordered the leaders of the Polish Communist underground to come to Moscow for "conversations." The jail sentence saved Gomulka's life because not one of his colleagues returned home. Accused of "Trotskyism," they were shot one by one on Stalin's orders.

"Historical necessity," Gomulka tried to explain to himself; he clenched his teeth and went on serving "the Cause." But the seed of resentment had been sown; it took roots and grew stronger, fanned by the traditional hatred of a Pole for the Russians.

Nineteen years later, during the ninth meeting of the Central Committee at Warsaw in May, 1957, he was attacked by several pro-Russian members of the Communist hierarchy and accused of leading Poland "away from the Russian orbit." He lashed back furiously and with painstaking details reminded his critics of how hundreds of Polish Communists, devoted to the policies of the Kremlin, had been mercilessly murdered by the Russians that tragic spring, exactly nineteen years ago. "Let it be a lesson and a warning to us and other Communists," he said with emotion.

This was the new Gomulka; but back in the days of the war, he still had a long way to go and much suffering lay before him.

He was in prison again when the Germans marched into Poland. When panic broke out, his jailers fled and he got out, destitute, with a serious lung ailment and a right knee stiffened by an old police bullet. In Warsaw he joined his wife Zofia, member of a Bolshevik family, and his son, who is now an engineer in Warsaw. He became a resistance fighter, a legend of bravery, whose daring acts of terrorism against the Germans commanded universal respect. In those days the common goal was victory. The legal Polish Government in London and more than 200,000 Polish soldiers outside Poland fought on the side of the United States and the British. Their plans were for an independent Poland politically and economically linked to the West. They were supported by a vast army of underground fighters inside Poland. Gomulka had a different objective: he too wanted the defeat of the Germans, but in his plans future Poland was to be closely allied with the Soviets. As a leader of the Communist underground and member of the Soviet-created Provisional Polish Government in Lublin, he took part in the Russian game of cruelty and deception. Together with Josef Stalin, whose orders he obediently carried out, he is responsible for the mass tragedy of the Warsaw uprising and for allowing the Russians to rule and exploit his country for more than a decade of horror. Serious crimes against Poland mar his record.

In 1946, as Deputy Premier and Secretary of the Communist United Workers' Party, he was at the zenith of his power. But something had been going on in his mind, setting him further and further apart from his colleagues. "I shall not allow Poland to become the seventeenth Soviet republic," he angrily told a gathering of peasants near Wroclaw. In 1948 he publicly denounced the ruinous policy of forced farm collectivization, and refused to condemn Tito's break with the Kremlin. Expelled from the Party in 1949, he was finally arrested in 1951 and would have been brought to trial and shot, had it not been for the death of Stalin in 1953.

His life had gone a full circle; it had been circumscribed
by his fanatical devotion to the "Cause"; there had been little
happiness, no room for personal joys, an unending procession of gray years, physical hardship, impaired health, danger
and solitary confinement. Why did he and the "Cause" come
to a parting of the ways? Because, as in all Poles, nationalism
in Gomulka is stronger than ideology. In 1948, when faced
with a choice between the good of Poland and a sacred Communist principle, he chose Poland. He chose it again last
October, and the nation rallied behind him. Their trust is
founded on the conviction that no matter what happens, Gomulka's course of action will remain nationalistic.

Looking in the direction of his bench, I saw him watch the
proceedings intently.

Although the business of the opening day was mostly or-
ganizational, the atmosphere in the chamber was lively. To
the audible delight of spectators in the crowded galleries,
several "nay" votes and abstentions were registered, when a
new Council of State was being elected on the floor. When
the former Prime Minister Joseph Cyrankiewicz was asked
to pick a new Cabinet, a tall, scholarly looking man rose to
protest the designation: "I regret," said Antoni Wojtysiak,
an Independent deputy from Legnica in southern Poland,
"but I am not going to vote for Mr. Cyrankiewicz. I have
no confidence in a man who has been Prime Minister during
the dark days of the Stalinist era; he is one of those we all
blame for the dismal condition of our country." There was
applause on the floor and excited chat in the galleries. Gomulka looked up from his bench, but there was no expression
on his face. It had been a long time since incidents such as
this used to occur in this room.

"Look at the TV cameras on the floor of the House," an
English newspaperman whispered excitedly behind me.

The scene in front of us was unusual. Half a dozen cameramen and assorted technicians were busily setting up equipment about ten feet away from where Gomulka and Cyrankiewicz were sitting. They turned on their spotlights and quietly proceeded to take pictures. Gomulka looked up quizzically. "This is CBS Radio, sir," said Ernest Leiser, CBS correspondent from Bonn. "I hope this does not disturb you; there is great interest in my country in this event." Gomulka did not answer, but smiled slightly.

"I expected some remonstrance or even to be escorted from the floor," Leiser later told me. "Gomulka did look a little pained before I finished, but he did not say anything. Hard to tell how free this Parliament is going to be, but it is encouraging to think that they allowed us to go through with a performance that would not have been tolerated in our own Congress, or even less in the Houses of Parliament in London."

During the intermission I talked to a woman deputy from Warsaw. A buxom, motherly blonde in her late forties, she addressed everybody as *"kochanie"* (darling). Elected last January on the Democratic Party ticket, she was one of the nineteen women in the 459-member Assembly. "The previous Sejm had sixty-eight women deputies," she said, "but most of them were there because of their Communist sympathies. This is different. I am here because I want decent schools in my district. Come back in a year, *kochanie*, and I shall report to you on my progress."

In the Sejm dining room a Catholic deputy—jovial, with a ruddy complexion—was having a glass of vodka with a Communist colleague; they were arguing a point heatedly, the Communist smilingly defending his thesis. Their conversation was lost in the general hum of the room, but they seemed to be on friendly, amiable terms.

In the white marble gallery upstairs, members of the government and high Party officials mingled freely with deputies,

diplomats and representatives of the press. I saw my friend
Mr. Putrament waving to me from the distance. He carried
a large sheaf of papers and looked busy. "I like your hat," he
said, examining my Lord & Taylor gray felt. "Are you having
a good time and have you met everybody you wanted?"

I pointed to a group where Gomulka and several Politburo
members were standing. "How about meeting *them?*" I whispered.

"Come," he said, and led me toward Cyrankiewicz, the
Prime Minister, whose tall, 200-pound figure and completely
bald head were like a landmark in the crowd. A long-time
Socialist, Cyrankiewicz had been frequently described as an
opportunist. "A professional swimmer," Warsaw wags said
of him. As Prime Minister in the days of the Stalin regime, he
had been a restraining if not always effective influence. Now
back in his old job, but in a different political climate, he
looked forward to again being able to dress and behave in
the manner of a Western gentleman.

He greeted me courteously and we chatted in Polish for a
while. But my attention was focused on the frail back of a
man who stood right next to him, engrossed in conversation.
He turned around suddenly and I found myself looking at
the steel-rimmed glasses and the thin, narrow lips of Wladyslaw Gomulka. His sallow, yellowish skin was sucked close
to the bones of his face; his nose sharp, and his ears dispro-
portionately large for the head, which was round with a fuzz
of white hair growing behind a receding forehead. What I
remember best of him at that moment are his eyes: grayish
blue—deeply set and mistrustful—the eyes of a man who has
suffered, who has been haunted by enemies and deceived by
his friends. A sad face—restless, but at the same time determined, with a steely, obstinate glint about it—primitive,
roughly hewn, with the watchful jerkiness of a man who has
never known inner peace.

"How come you speak Polish so well?" he asked, looking straight through me without smiling.

I explained my history and the circumstances that led to the trip. He looked interested and asked how long I planned to remain in the country. "You haven't forgotten the language," he said; his voice was flat with fatigue; he smiled slightly and turned to hear the report of an aide.

"Are they right, those who trust him?" I wondered, looking at the closed, inscrutable face. He represented the change that the Poles had so passionately desired, but much of his power was due to circumstances. Without his nation's revulsion at the Russian controls and their bitterness born of long years of misery, Gomulka would not have happened. He was the catalyst who channeled the scattered sparks into action. Of his deep mistrust of Russia there is no doubt. His love for Poland is profound, but as a Communist he is inwardly shackled by the restrictive maze of a vicious and arrogant doctrine. He has come a long way from the days of his blind belief in Marxian dogmas, but much of the Communist core still remains. He believes that his regime must be based on the Party, and that adherence to the Party line is essential. Those who refuse to toe it will be shunted; not jailed, or punished, or blacklisted—such methods belong to the past— just replaced by others, who comply.

"Absolute freedom is a luxury in which we cannot afford to indulge," he replied, when asked about press censorship. His immediate argument is that it would provoke Russia, but it is a big question whether Gomulka, who himself has never known real freedom, realizes what a precious possession it is. Therein lies a potential source of conflict with his people. The nation's desire for freedom keeps growing; Party slogans mean nothing. The present membership of the Communist Party in Poland is anyone's guess. While aware of the Russian menace, the Poles will not give up the gains they earned last October. They want more—and a better standard of living.

Will this tortuous, solitary man, caught in an ideological dilemma, be able to satisfy them? Or will they sweep him away, discontented—thus inviting Russian intervention?

Gomulka moved away from the group. I went in and watched the proceedings till the end. In the downstairs lobby of the Sejm a huge map of Poland occupied a whole wall; a vast, uninterrupted plain stretched from Warsaw all the way to Moscow. The "invasion" route, it used to be called in our school-books. I retrieved my coat and went out. The first session of the post-October Sejm was over.

CHAPTER 6

An Armful of Jasmin

THE voice at the other end of the wire sounded familiar: "This is Lucio speaking. I heard you were in Warsaw—sensational news! How long are you going to be here, and when could one see you?"

Lucio was a neighbor of ours in the country and one of my earliest beaus. He had a country place near us, and I had known him ever since I could remember.

He was a good fifteen years older than I was, but the fact that he had reached his thirties still unmarried had lent him additional glamor. He had a great way with the ladies. Knowing that he was one of the most eligible bachelors in the country, he usually concentrated his attentions on married women where, as he said, there was less of a danger of being hooked. His farms were run at a profit; he was good-looking, an exceptionally good sportsman and a first-rate bridge player —qualities that made him popular with my father.

I remember him driving up the circular driveway to our house at the wheel of his blue convertible named *"l'Oiseau Bleu,"* which was known all over Poland for its speed, foreign gadgets and the gaiety of its occupants.

Lucio paid a lot of attention to me at my coming-out party the summer I was seventeen. He even invited me to his house for the annual pheasant shoot in November, an honor eagerly coveted by most of my contemporaries.

The fact that I was very young did not matter much in those days. With daughters in the house, it was a good idea to line up prospective husbands early; in fact, the earlier a girl married, the better, it was generally felt. The husband was supposed to have the proper family background and some money, which usually meant landholdings in our world; the girl was expected to bring a nice dowry. But the primary object of marriage was, after all, to have children. A married woman in those days was supposed to produce five to six children. Wives trying to evade this responsibility were severely condemned by the Church.

I liked Lucio. Whenever he came to see us, he spent most of his time discussing horses with Father or Warsaw gossip with Mother. I don't remember ever spending more than five minutes alone with him, but his attention flattered my ego. It was only when he made a formal request for my hand (he arrived one day all dressed up and locked himself in a room with my father) that I realized that the very last thing I wanted was to become a matron—not just yet. There were too many other things I wanted to do first. I was having a lovely time in my last school year in Paris; I was anxious to travel, go to England and generally have some fun. I did not envy my cousins who, married at eighteen, had little to look forward to but more children. There will always be time enough to settle in the country and be married, I decided.

I discussed the whole matter with my wonderful father, who was fun-loving as well as wise, and we decided that I should go on with my studies.

Lucio was disappointed, but he consoled himself by proposing to a schoolmate of mine a few months later. We remained excellent friends; I was one of the bridesmaids at their

wedding, which took place a few weeks before the outbreak
of war.

That was the last time I saw him. I heard that he had spent
the war in a German prisoner-of-war camp, that he had been
divorced and that he had remarried when he returned home
after the war.

Now, going downstairs to meet him, I thought of the
different world we had found ourselves in after eighteen
years. It made the old days seem unreal.

He was sitting in one of the red plush armchairs in the hall
looking toward the stairway. He rose with a wide, cheerful
smile and gave me an affectionate hug. He seemed taller and
grayer, but as gay and cheerful as ever.

"We are not going to lunch here," he declared. "The food
at the Bristol is the end. I shall take you to Rarytas; it is con-
siderably better."

We climbed into a hiccuping little taxi, an Opel of the 1923
vintage, and proceeded to Rarytas, the town's fanciest eating
establishment. There was a doorman in a navy-blue and red
uniform, an imposing staircase and an array of tables covered
with white tablecloths. Waiters hovered among them in the
best capitalist tradition.

We ordered smoked Russian salmon and vodka to start
with, then jugged Polish hare in sour cream with red beets.

Lucio lifted his vodka glass. "Here is to your visit to
Poland, and to the United States for keeping you looking so
well. You know," he laughed, "I was terribly curious to see
you and I rather expected that you would be unrecognizable.
I don't mean better or worse looking, but sort of completely
foreign and different. I am glad you retained a substantial
part of yourself. I feel that eighteen years is not a long time
after all."

For my part, I thought *he* looked remarkably well. There
was the same gay twinkle and the quick appraising glance at

the ladies, and the commanding manner of the wealthy landowner used to having his wishes complied with.

"You manage to adjust yourself very well to the socialist
system," I said, observing the unusual speed with which the
waiters carried out his commands.

"This is not a bad restaurant," he said, "though State-
owned, as everything else is these days. But the waiters here
are old-timers; they like to do things the right way. The
trouble is that not enough customers care or demand it be
done. The people who have money these days do not care
what they eat, as long as the vodka is there."

I was longing to learn what he did with himself, how he
had managed to stay afloat after everything he had owned
had been taken away from him. I remembered the lovely old
house, the carefully tended grounds, the thousands of acres
of forest, and the rich, rolling farmlands made fertile by the
care and knowledge lavished on them by generations of
scientific farming. This was all divided, parceled out, given
in bits to the peasants or taken over abruptly by the State
for one of its badly managed agricultural experimental stations.

"When did you last see Tulikowo?" I inquired. This was
the house he lived in.

"In the summer of 1945 I returned from the prisoner-of-
war camp and went straight home. I took a train from Warsaw to Turek, the nearest town, then hired a taxi. But I was
not allowed to stay in the house. The Party delegate had got
there before me. Nothing was mine any more; it was all 'their
property' now, including my personal belongings. Some of
the furniture had been taken west by the Germans, but most
of the heavy pieces remained. My pictures and my silver were
still there, and I dug out the fur-lined rugs from a cache in
the garden. I had quite a collection of them. Do you remember?"

I remembered the bright winter days, the horse-driven sleighs in the snow-covered forest, the comfort and warmth of the fox-lined rugs, and the exhilaration that came from the mixture of speed, brilliant sun and the snow.

"How did the people on the place behave when you arrived?"

"It varied greatly," said Lucio. "Most of my personal servants left in the early days of the war, when the house was a German command post. The peasants themselves were divided. Owning their own piece of land was, of course, a glittering prospect; but the joy of anticipation was marred by the uncertainty of how permanent it was going to be. Those getting the arable land were pleased, but what were some of them to do with a dozen of acres of forest? They of course still had the houses I had built for them on the place. There was talk of converting the big house into small dwelling units for the village, but they had no livestock, no machines and no means of communication on the place. Some of them looked defiant and some sheepish: all were amazed and quite scared when I suddenly turned up. I left as I came—in a taxi. I had no money to live on, but I felt that some remnants of the old style should be preserved."

"Did you take anything with you when you left?"

"It was a very strange situation. Here I stood, with one wornout suit to my name, still wearing my Army shoes, looking into the huge closet in my bedroom—pilfered, but still with a few sport jackets and some excellent pairs of shoes in it. I saw my camel-hair coat I had bought in London years ago and which now represented a fortune. Still, I felt their eyes upon me. They had been told by the Party representative that it was all *theirs*. They were ashamed and uncertain, but greed was all over their faces.

"I looked at Maran, the foreman whose two sons I had put

through college. I was curious as to whether he would say anything, but he turned his head sheepishly.

"I closed the door and went out, climbed back into the taxi and departed. I shall never go there again.

"After that, I lived in Warsaw for some time. Then I decided to try my luck in the new western territories Poland got back from the Germans. I ran a successful tool business in Wroclaw until early in 1952, when the government decided that it was going too well and expropriated me overnight. I was not the only one. That was a fast Stalinist rule: 'The worse individual enterprises are going, the better it is for the State.' It affected every successful businessman in those days. Private initiative on all levels had to be stamped out ruthlessly. As a result, the newly acquired lands which used to be prosperous and well managed became an economic desert. It will take at least twenty years to repair the damage of this lunatic policy.

"I returned to Warsaw and tried to make a living. I managed a State-owned restaurant for a while, ran a brewery business for a State concern. Now I am getting ready to open a vegetable-processing plant of my own. I can employ up to thirty people in it, and it could be successful. Everything is much easier since October. There is plenty of confusion around, but the mental climate is quite different. I feel like starting something again. After all, one has to be versatile in *our* era."

I admired his elasticity. Here was a man brought up in great wealth, schooled in the ways of running a thousand-acre estate and vast armies of workers, secure in a way of life that had remained unchanged for hundreds of years, who bounced back smiling, and who at the age of fifty-four had willingly adjusted himself to starting a new life from nothing.

"It has been easier for me than for most of the older ones," he told me. "Many of your parents' friends simply could not take it. They are scattered all over. Many have gone abroad; some are living in towns with their children; others have jobs of some kind. For years they have been blacklisted, but now a 'reactionary' name does not seem to matter any more.

"Do you remember Grabowski, the prominent horseman, who was a good friend of your father's? He manages the largest State-owned stud farm in Pomerania. It is an ideal job for him, and he has had it for some years. They were reluctant to give it to him at first, but they were finally forced to, as no other man in Poland knows so much about horses as old Janek. Few, of course, were as lucky as he was.

"Take Severyn Czerakowski, right here in Warsaw. After being in prison for four years because he happened to be called Czerakowski, he was recently named chairman of the committee for the reconstruction of the Europejski Hotel. As you know, he had built the Europejski before the war, owned and ran it successfully for over twenty years. But he is pleased with the nomination and got to work on the plans right away. Next time you come to Warsaw you may be staying at the Europejski, if all goes well."

"Any hope of his ever owning it again?"

"I doubt it," said Lucio. "It is a pretty big business and it probably would be hard to fit it into the framework of the new socialist state we are supposed to be building." He laughed. "But who knows? It is a tremendous step forward, their letting him plan and run it."

We ate in silence for a while.

"Will you go to Szczypiorno?" he asked. "Don't! It will only depress you." Szczypiorno was the name of the place where we lived before the war.

"I am going there next Thursday," I told him. "It has been on my mind ever since I arrived here. I simply have got to see it—if only to put the memories to rest."

"I drove through it a year ago," said Lucio. "I tell you that you are going to be very depressed and angry when you see it. The rascals made a shambles of it. They destroyed a flourishing place and derived no benefits from the process. Now nobody has got anything. Very sound economics, indeed!"

"I wonder if any of the old-timers are still there," I said. "I would like to know what *they* think."

"Nothing much, you will find," replied Lucio. "The old ones would like us all to come back, I am sure. The young ones like it this way, basically, now that they can own their own land. Give my best to Teodor, the butler, if you see him. What a wonderful butler he was! No one could press a suit or put a shine on a shoe as well as he did. For years I tried to steal him away from your father."

"He was a great admirer of yours, I remember. He always tried to tell me you were the ideal husband for me."

We laughed, dozens of memories rushing suddenly to the surface.

"You see how wise you were that you waited? You would not be looking so well had you spent the last eighteen years in Poland. It has been much tougher on the women than on the men. Still, our Polish women manage to look pretty well, considering what they've been through."

We walked out of the restaurant into the late afternoon. We had been lunching for over three hours.

"Let me know when you come back from Szczypiorno," said Lucio.

I turned into Marszalkowska Street and walked all the way back to the Bristol. I was deep in memories of my childhood; it seemed as if I had never left Poland. . . .

I remember the red rambler roses climbing over the south side of the house. They came up to our tall nursery windows, and we tried to lean over and pick them during our afternoon naptime. We were not permitted to do it and were pulled back by our pigtails when caught.

Sophie, my sister, was blond—almost white-haired—with enormous blue eyes. She had a lovely, shy smile and liked dolls and sad fairy stories. I was older than she; my hair was light chestnut and curly, and I liked horses and books. Later, a brother arrived. He was given the family name of Ian, but we called him Yasiek. Telegrams of congratulations "on the continuation of the line" arrived at the house by the dozen. It was the happy event my mother had been praying for for some years. Her first two born had been daughters—always much less an achievement than a son. My arrival, in particular, was a big disappointment. Since a son was definitely counted on, no girl's name had even been selected for me. I remained unnamed for a month. I owe my name of Christine to a friend of my mother's, who happened to turn up at the house. I was named after her with the hope that someday I would grow to be as gay and attractive as she was.

To thank God for a son, a private chapel was built at the end of the alley of pink chestnuts, at the very edge of the park; and a Mass was said there every Sunday by a visiting priest from Kalisz, the neighboring town. The entire village and all the farm people attended. We always drove to the chapel in an open horse carriage, sitting straight and quite solemn in our starched Sunday dresses, on the narrow back seat, facing Mother, smiling and beautiful, with a long, flowing hat veil falling softly behind her.

We sat in our special pew near the altar; it had high crimson pillows I liked. Our arrival was usually timed for "just after the sermon," because the blunt language of the country priest—who liked to upbraid the peasants for drinking and more serious sins—was deemed unsuitable for our ears. Now and then the clergyman would fool us and deliver the sermon right in the middle of the service. It made a dignified exit impossible. Some of my earliest glimpses into the facts of life came from overhearing our preachers.

I remember the house as one came upon it after a long, winding drive between clipped hedges of yew and hazel bushes. It lay among the lime trees and the oaks planted two centuries ago, now splendid in their maturity. It was a white stone house, three-storied, with terraces and steps leading down to a pond called "The Lake." Green lawns and flower beds surrounded it on all sides. In the distance lay fields of wheat and of barley and a vast expanse of parklike meadowland where thoroughbred horses were grazing.

The house was built late in the 18th century, after a great-great-grandfather of mine moved the family place there from Silesia. It remained untouched through the wars, successive national uprisings, World War I and the tumultuous period of the Bolshevik invasion in the early twenties. During World War I, a German garrison was stationed on the place for months; but no harm was done to the house, the grounds or even the flowers. Those were the civilized days when, for civilians living behind enemy lines, wars were a distant contest with little effect on their lives. My grandmother used to recall the well-mannered, heel-clicking German general who came to apologize to her because his soldiers had killed several of her prizewinning turkeys.

The next war was to be fought differently, but we did not know it—as yet.

There were over thirty rooms in the house, with tall windows deeply framed in thick walls. I remember the entrance hall with its forest of buck horns fastened to little tablets of wood. It led to a huge L-shaped room with a wide fireplace and old prints. Beyond it was the main drawing room with French doors opening onto a terrace and gardens.

We children lived on the first floor of the house in what was generally referred to as "the rooms behind the mirror," because one came there through a door hidden behind an immense antique mirror. I remember the metric scale on the other side of this door with pencil marks studiously recording our growth. A paneled passage led to my parents' bedrooms. On the way was our favorite hiding place—the largest closet I have ever seen. It was built into the thickness of the wall, the size of a large room. It saved the life of my grandfather who fought the Russians in the Polish 1863 uprising. He spent a week in it, hiding from the police of the Tsars, who searched the house unsuccessfully to lead him away to Siberia. The extraordinary depth of the closet saved him.

Below us, in the basement, spread the land of the kitchens, the pantries, the bakery and wine cellars. It was the kingdom of Mr. Tchepek, the cook, an eccentric and irascible man, but a master of his art. The food was pulled up from the kitchen by way of a dumbwaiter to the pantry outside the dining-room door and then brought up to the table. It was an efficient arrangement if the dining-room servants were fast at pulling it up, but sometimes Mr. Tchepek would explode in a rage that his art was being ruined by their slowness.

At the close of the First World War, when my parents were married, electricity was installed in the house, the village and the adjoining farm buildings. Later one always talked about putting in central heating. One day an expert was called who declared that the heat would ruin the delicate parquet floors brought in by my grandfather from Dresden. We children were very happy that the white porcelain stoves, built flat into the walls and decorated with cheerful Renaissance puttis, would be left unchanged in their place. They were warm and cozy and comfortable to lean against. We could not imagine the house without them. One of the most familiar sounds linked to the days of my childhood was the early-morning stoking of the fires in the winter. One used to open one's eyes,

turn over and go back to sleep happily with the familiar
warmth spreading throughout the room.

On most mornings when my father was home, Witek, the
groom, dressed in his dark-blue livery coat, waited in front
of the house with a tall carriage which was called "The American." No one ever knew why. It had a wide, high, front
seat and a narrow one in the back for the groom, and it was
pulled by a pair of matched horses in gleaming harness decorated with the family crest. I loved nothing more than to
sit next to Father, way above the high-stepping harmonious
animals and at a spanking pace pass through the gates of the
park, way down the acacia-bordered road to the farm. Depending on the time of the year, we would stop to look over
the last sowings, the new planting or confer with the foreman
over the yield of grain from the harvest. I would hold the
reins a little anxiously, under the stern eye of the groom,
while Father conferred on the ground.

Now and then, on formal occasions like a big shoot, a
flower show or a wedding, Father drove a perfectly matched
four-in-hand. It was tricky to control the horses, which could
be hardly held back, but there was no more beautiful sight.

I was fortunate to have as my parents two people about
whom it was said that they were one of the most attractive
couples in the country. Father was not only a brilliant agricultural expert, a summa-cum-laude graduate of the tough
University of Munich, an outstanding breeder of fine horses,
a man of great political wisdom who served his country well
during its brief period of independence, but also a witty,
amusing companion, good-looking, with a tremendous fondness for living. He did everything in broad strokes, disliked
wavering and small details—he was imaginative and daring,
and nearly always successful. In Poland, where the 20th century had not really taken hold, he was the embodiment of the

enlightened landowner, perfectly used to command, but conscious of what was expected of him.

He married my mother when she was only eighteen. There was more than ten years' difference between them; but as Mother's beauty developed, so did their love and pride in each other. They traveled and entertained a very wide circle of friends, but they were always pleased to be ultimately left alone with each other.

We children grew in an atmosphere of rocklike security, following a way of life unchanged for centuries. As modern harvesters began to arrive at the farm, newer and more modern bathrooms were put into the house; brick living quarters were built for the villagers and farmhands, but our essential way of life remained the same. We rode around on our ponies, played with the children of the village—our friends—paid daily visits to the stables and the farm, and followed the cycle of the seasons. The house had stood there for a long time; the family had always been in it; one day we would grow up and get married and Ian, our brother, would live there. Nothing could change—so we thought.

It was a good life. When I look back at it now, it seems full of anachronisms, but its roots grew deep in ancient soil. When the change-over came, it was brutal. The country is still recovering from the shock that followed its violence.

By the standards of his day, my father was a wealthy man. His income came from the soil, from the scientific way he administered his close-to-three-thousand acres of land. There were two properties: Szczypiorno, where we lived, with acres of orchards, meadows, plantations of hop, an experimental seed farm, water mills, fisheries, and one of the best stud farms in Poland; and Russew, some fifteen miles away, famous for its rich black soil and record crops of sugar beet, wheat and barley.

Father's hobby was horses. They were his constant joy and

excitement. He traveled throughout Europe visiting renowned studs and racing stables and knew the history and blood lines of every prominent race horse in Europe. By crossing the thoroughbred English mare with the delicate Arab stallion, he was the first in Poland to develop a new Anglo-Arab strain famous for its stamina and grace. This proved a more felicitous combination than the hitherto-practiced crossing of the thoroughbred English stallion with an Arabian mare.

Father could tell the worth of a horse at a glance. "There is no nobler creation in the animal kingdom than a horse," he would remark, observing fondly a particularly successful yearling.

"Getting the horses to bed" was a sport that we especially enjoyed. Each day toward the evening they had to be rounded up in the paddocks and galloped at full speed along the tree-lined country road back toward the stables for the night. It was a choice distinction to be able to ride bareback like the grooms all the way from the paddocks to home. I remember passing the sun on the way, setting behind the oak trees near the house, and Father, tall and erect, standing against a stone pillar with a walking stick in his hand, watching all of us gallop by.

When I was ten years old, I was sent to a boarding school about two hundred miles north of home. It was a very nice place on a lake, and I enjoyed being there, glad to get away from the various governesses who, having taught me how to read and write, now concentrated on my younger sister and brother.

The first vacation of the school year was for All Saints' Day in November—just in time for the annual pheasant shoot, which was always exciting. For days before the date of the shoot, Father and the forester drew plans indicating locations where the individual huntsmen would stand. There were usually about twelve of them, and only "good shots" were invited. Everyone got up early on the day of the shoot and met in the dining room for breakfast. Felt boots, extra sweaters, fur gloves and mufflers were put on, guns slung over the shoulders, pockets filled with cartridges. Each man, followed by a servant with the second gun and extra boxes of cartridges, piled into one of the waiting carriages outside and proceeded to the position assigned to him by the forester. Positions were changed with each beat, so that everyone had a reasonable chance to kill birds. Beaters came from villages within a twenty-mile radius. Most of them were high-school children paid about ten cents for their labors—not a bad income in those days.

I remember the pale light of those late autumn days and the haze that clung over the thickets of tall firs as the distant shouts, tappings and whistlings of the beaters filled the air between the huntsmen and their prey. Then a loud bustle of wings would suddenly come from somewhere in the undergrowth as the red-rusty pheasants flew upward, topping the highest trees in their speed. Loud shouts of "Tiro!" would follow, and all down the line there would be a frantic explosion of guns. Bodies of birds would rain down, landing everywhere with dull plops. Now and then a loud swearing was heard, directed at a servant who had failed to reload a gun fast enough. When the beaters came out into sight, the first stand would be over.

Some years, a total of over a thousand cocks was thus brought down in a day. Some men managed to kill as many as 120 in one morning. I liked the atmosphere of the shoot and the trappings that usually went with it. Lunch was usually brought out into the fields and served in a rapidly rigged pavilion with a roof of fat pine-tree branches. Back in school, I liked to compare notes and see whether our records were excelled.

One of my favorite huntsmen was Walewski, a distant

neighbor, whom we liked to visit in the summer during our riding excursions. He lived with his family in an enchanting old house which to us was steeped in romance. It was the family seat of Maria Walewska, Napoleon's "Polish wife," the most romantic figure in the history of 19th-century Poland. Since history has curtly described her as his mistress and technically she was no more, the Walewskis did not point to the connection with pride. Her portrait, made by Nattier, decorated their living room; but one had to insist to be told whose identity it revealed. For over 125 years the family had been struggling with the problem of what official line to adopt regarding the unorthodox conduct of their beautiful ancestress: "Should we be proud of her—or ashamed?" The question was tough to resolve.

Marie Walewska was nineteen when, on January 1, 1807, she met the Emperor of the French. She had been married for four years to Count Anastase Colonna-Walewski, who was seventy and had been married twice before. According to records of the period, she was "pure, pious, passionately patriotic —and exquisite to look at." Coulaincourt's memoirs describe her as "an angelic person, with a skin like a pink rose, big, blue, soft, innocent eyes, the gaiety and the grace of a gazelle."

Poland's name had disappeared from the map of Europe. Since 1795, the country had been partitioned between the Austrian, Prussian and Russian empires. Maria, the fervent patriot, prayed every day for a saviour who would restore independence to Poland. The legend of Bonaparte was already sweeping through Poland. Here was the heir to the French Revolution, the standard-bearer of freedom, the military genius who had defeated an Austro-Russian alliance at Austerlitz and was now prepared to wage a war against Prussia. Polish volunteers under Dabrowski had been fighting for Napoleon in Italy and Egypt, and he was known to have said at Verona only a short time before: "I like the Poles. The partition of Poland was an iniquitous deed, that cannot stand. When I have finished the war in Italy, I will lead the French myself and force the Russians to re-establish Poland."

Now he was coming to Warsaw. The timid little countess had a reckless impulse. She would be the first one to salute the great man. She jumped into a carriage and drove about ten miles out of Warsaw, west to the little village of Blonie, where the Emperor halted to change horses. Her carriage stopped next to that of General Duroc, Grand Marshal of the Household and Napoleon's close friend. In her impeccable French, Maria asked to be taken to the Emperor. Charmed by her beauty, Duroc led her to Napoleon's carriage door. She was so shy and blushing that she could hardly utter a word, but the effect of her beauty on Napoleon was electric. He drove to Warsaw and demanded to see her again.

Now Polish statesmen decided that the future fate of the country lay in the hands of the little Maria. She was urged and implored to give in to Napoleon's advances. Even her aged husband declared that "she owed it to her country."

Maria's stiff religious upbringing fought against her equally strong patriotism. What if by giving herself to the great military hero she ensured future independence to Poland? She was only nineteen: an Emperor was pursuing her with the whole country, even her husband, on his side, she finally consented to see him alone in his palace one night naively imagining that perhaps he would respect her, understand her, give her his friendship and trust, and listen to her prayers for Poland. They would end up by becoming good friends—nothing else. . . .

Things turned out differently. She first submitted to the conqueror's embrace with resignation, thinking always of Poland; but she soon had to admit to herself that her patriotic duties were not unpleasant. As weeks in Warsaw went by, she fell deeply in love with Napoleon; it was an enduring

love that was to last all her life. He took her to Paris with
him, where three years later their son Alexandre was born.
(He was to win fame as Minister of Foreign Affairs under
Napoleon III.) He tenderly referred to her in his letters as
"my Polish wife." She was the only woman that he had really
loved—the only one he knew who never wanted anything for
herself. Maria remained by his side when everything else col-
lapsed around him and followed him into exile to the island
of Elba.

Coulaincourt recalls in his memoirs that Napoleon toyed
with the idea of marrying Maria after his divorce from Jose-
phine became final. But political considerations—and the
snobbery of the Corsican rebel—prevailed. He married the
daughter of the Austrian Emperor instead, declaring he had
to have a son who would be the child of a princess of royal
blood. "My little cabbage," he would say to Maria, "if only
your blood were as royal as your beauty!"

But the future turned against him. After the disintegration
of the Empire, his royal wife left him, taking away their son
to be brought up as an Austrian prince. The pathetic little
Duke of Reichstadt died at an early age without ever ful-
filling the promises of his birth. Only Maria Walewska
remained: to her, he was "her Napoleon"; she loved him tenderly for himself.

Such was the story of the beautiful Countess Maria. To us,
it was always enthralling. I remember how one day a particularly vivid book on the subject disappeared from the library
shelves at home. It came back a few days later with several
pages clipped together by Mother. We were not supposed
to read it.

One day in August 1939, returning home from a ride in
the fields, we found several Polish officers in the house. All
that summer the political situation had been growing steadily

worse; a war with Germany seemed imminent. The officers came to talk to my father about the evacuation of horses. The Szczypiorno stud was a valuable reservoir of military remount horses; they should be sent east, across the country close to the Russian border, where they would be safe from the Germans. Father reluctantly consented to have part of the stud moved to Polesie, on the eastern border of Poland. The horses got there safely, but barely two weeks after the beginning of the war they were taken over by the Russians, who occupied the country from the east, joining hands with the advancing German armies.

On Friday, September 1, a hazy, late summer day, I awoke to hear bombs falling into the flower beds on the grounds. Silvery German planes, with Polish markings deceivingly painted over their wings, flew low over the house, machine-gunning people working out in the fields, dropping bombs on the farm and setting acres of woodland afire. There had been no official declaration of war, but obviously this was it. We were about 180 miles from Berlin, less than 25 miles from the German border, but such was the widespread confidence in the fighting quality and the might of the Polish Army that few of us worried about the outcome of the conflict. "We shall crush them," said the announcer over the Polish radio that morning, as regiments of dashing Polish cavalrymen with glistening sabres prepared to take up positions against an avalanche of armored German tanks and unending waves of Luftwaffe planes.

Since it was evident that we were going to be occupied any moment, the family decided to go to Warsaw to wait for the end of the conflict. "It will be a drawn-out affair," it was said. "It may be better to sit it out in Warsaw." The reasoning was still along the lines of the First World War.

I was anxious to do something and together with a few friends joined a volunteer clerical unit attached to the Polish

General Staff. Our job was to translate foreign broadcasts, particularly those of our allies, the French and the British; but before we had time to do any work, the full-scale retreat of the Polish armies had begun.

"If we get separated, try to get back to France and finish school," said my father. He was sitting in a deep leather armchair in a room at the Bristol Hotel in Warsaw, where we all met for a while. He was visibly gray at the temples. His fine, straight features showed strain; there were deep fatigue wrinkles around the calm blue eyes that I loved. That was the last time I saw him.

When the Russian armies moved in, the road to Warsaw was closed. Together with family friends, I crossed into Rumania. I was then put on the Orient Express and sent to Paris, where I disembarked three days later. The school year was just starting; France was officially in the war, but it was several months before the war became active. Life resumed its normal routine again.

My parents settled in Lowicz, a town not very far from Warsaw, waiting for the war to end. They were not allowed to return to Szczypiorno, which had now become the residence of the governor of the province of Wartegau, named after the river Warta, which flowed there. It was a German name, and the whole province was incorporated into the German Reich. My parents were confident, however, that they would return before long. The family had always gone back in the past. But this time it was not to be so: this was a different war—one that brought revolution in its wake.

A year before the end of the war, Father died, without seeing his home. My younger sister and brother fought in the ill-fated Warsaw uprising. They had remained in Poland with my parents. My brother Ian was only sixteen when he joined General Bor's Home Army to fight for the liberation of Warsaw. He was killed by German shrapnel at short range, while trying to make his way through the rubble-strewn streets and the network of sewers to deliver a message to his unit. It was nine years before his body was found.

When the Home Army surrendered, Zosia, my blond-pigtailed sister, was sent to a prisoner-of-war camp near Hanover, where I found her eight months later when, following Montgomery's advance, we crossed into Germany from England with the British Red Cross. She was thin but unharmed, and quite cheerful. She asked to be taken to the hairdresser's in Brussels.

Only Mother was now left in Poland. At the end of the war, she returned to the house, but the Party delegate had been there before her. "The land now belongs to the peasants," she was told. "So do the *dwor* (the manor house) and the grounds and the livestock. Nothing is to be taken out."

The new law stipulated that no former landowner was ever to reside closer than a fifty-mile radius from his former property. "The morale of the new, *rightful* owners is not to be disturbed," it read.

Within a year Szczypiorno was turned into a collective farm. Eighteen families moved into the house; the paddocks were plowed under; the orchards, the fields, the carefully planted grounds—all became part of *kolkhoz* No. 287.

"We possess nothing certainly—except our past." I thought of the Greek philosopher's words on that mild spring afternoon in May, 1957, as I was driving back to the house for the first time since I left it a few days after the outbreak of war.

For the last eighteen years, my memories had lain dormant; they carried a shadowy existence in my mind, because there was so little relation between them and the life I was leading. The world of my childhood had come to an end with the war; the one in which I became an adult was like a totally different planet. I liked it—and seldom missed the first half of my life. It seemed like a charming anachronism when viewed from the perspective of my Manhattan apartment. Now I was going back, driving along the main highway from Poznan in an apple-green American Chevrolet belonging to Ed Symans, of the American Embassy in Warsaw. Only a few days before I had said to a Communist deputy, "I am going home to see what you have done to my land. I shall see how your theories work when applied to a place I know well."

"Oh, you are a reactionary, I know." He laughed, amused and very good-natured, and he invited me to tell him all about it when I returned.

"Do you recognize anything?" asked Therese Symans, who was sitting next to me in the car. She was terribly excited for me.

"Yes. There will be a turn to the left in a moment, and we shall drive through a forest," I said without hesitation. We were about thirty miles from the house. Details were falling back into place in my mind like a jigsaw puzzle.

We were driving through rich parklike country. On both sides of the road, fields of yellow clover spread like a festive carpet. This was Poznanskie, the province of Poznan, where land cultivation was the highest in Poland. A forest of fir trees closed in around us. "Soon we should see the walls of the Czartoryski Museum at Goluchow," I said subconsciously, as the forest tapered off to a clearing.

As if in a miracle, a red-brick wall came into view. There was a large bulletin board at the gates, stating the visiting hours and the lectures; but the magnificent house which became a museum shortly before the outbreak of war seemed unchanged from the distance.

"Jedlec—4 km.," said a sign pointing to a poplar-lined sandy road. "I really should stop off and see Stefan's house," I thought. "It would be nice to write him in London about it."

Stefan Zamoyski was a neighbor of ours and a friend of my father's. They used to discuss horses for days, and Father sometimes admitted that Stefan knew almost as much about them as he did. But we had to go on.

Presently the town of Kalisz—our capital, we used to call it—came into view: a picturesque country town on the River Prosna. It was known for its fine baroque churches, one of which claimed to have a genuine Rubens in the sanctuary. We took a shortcut through the town and came out on the other side, by a cemetery, where the smooth pavement changed into cobblestones. I remembered the spot very well. As one came onto it in a horse-driven carriage, the rhythmic sound of horseshoes instantly became heavier as the cobblestones came under the horses' hoofs. Sometimes, coming home late, we would fall asleep in the carriage and wake up precisely at that moment. We then knew exactly where we were.

We were now running parallel to the railroad tracks. Thirty-five years before, when an extension of the Warsaw-Poznan railroad link was to be built through the edge of our property, my father had the Ministry's plans revised according to his own specifications, so that the tracks would not interfere with Mother's plans for a new avenue of trees. A tiny station was built on our place, and the Warsaw express stopped on a telephoned request whenever one of the family was traveling.

We now passed under the railroad bridge and turned off. The familiar driveway lay winding before us. "How the box hedges have grown! They need clipping," I thought. The orchards spread on both sides, heavy with fruit, as before. Only the forest of peaches was not there—they used to look like a sea of pink petals every spring. I learned later that frost had killed them all off gradually. At the next bend of the road, the oak trees came into view and I saw two horses and a cow grazing where the lawns used to be. Now the house

appeared in the distance—white and bigger than I remembered. "It does have graceful proportions," I thought, feeling
curiously detached and objective. The water in the lake was
high; the spring must have been a wet one. The crunch of
the gravel was familiar as we swept onto the circular terrace.
I got out of the car and looked.

The house wore deep wounds on its face; its scars stared
at me helplessly. The right side of the balustrade was gone;
weeds grew all over the flagstones, and there were two gaping holes in the terrace. The yew trees in front of the house,
clipped in conical shapes by the gardeners, were now brown,
with branches falling down to the ground. The glass in many
windows was missing, and they were boarded with planks.
I looked up to the left, where my parents' rooms used to be,
and saw a line of washing floating out of the wide window
frame. The house was obviously being lived in. There were
papers and broken bottles all around.

A peasant woman carrying a bucket of water in each hand
came hurrying across the lawn. Another came out of the
house and stared. "Jesus Maria!" she shouted. "*Panienka
Krysia* is here (the young Miss Christine)!" She ran toward
me and stopped short. "Don't you recognize me?" she asked.
"I am Hanusia. I used to work in the manor laundry for
years. Irka, your maid, is here, and Wojtasik, the gardener,
and Yanka, daughter of Kaziulek, the coachman. God! Wait,
I must tell them all right now!" She ran into the house yell-
ing.

Now all the windows flew open; the door became
crammed with people. More arrived on the terrace, and I
found myself standing in the middle of an enormous crowd.
An old man wearing crinkled black-leather boots pushed his
way through the crowd, bent down low and kissed my hand
solemnly.

"May Jesus Christ be praised," he said.

"Forever and ever," I automatically answered. This was the familiar greeting of the village people I knew well. I looked at him and said, "Wojtasik," a little hesitantly.

He beamed. *"Yasna panienka* (the brightly illuminated miss) has recognized old Wojtasik. I have been here all along —the Germans, the Russians, and the *kolkhoz.* And now we are on our own. I still take care of the orchards; they are now under the State Fruit Cooperative in Kalisz. But I have been quite sick lately. . . ." He looked old and seemed to be limping slightly.

The others in the crowd were staring at me without words. They looked poor and bedraggled. The men wore tattered workshirts. Hanusia's blue-denim skirt showed signs of frequent repairs and hard wear; she had on a pair of wooden sandals called "trepy." Back in the days of my childhood, only the poorest wore trepy.

"Wojtasik," I asked, "how many of you live in the house at the moment?"

"Twenty-three families," he replied. "It has all been changed around and partitioned. We were told to move in when the land was given to us. You know"—he looked at me hesitantly—"my wife and I have your old room upstairs, the one that was all done up for you when you came home from school that last summer."

I remembered my "coming-out present," the great event of moving to one of the large guest rooms upstairs, which had been redecorated for me in flowered chintz, with soft tones of green and ivory on the walls. Next to it was a small sitting room where I could entertain my friends.

"I would like to have a look at my room," I said to Wojtasik. "Let's go!"

At the left of the entrance, where the hall used to be, stood an enormous porcelain bathtub. It looked sad and forlorn, sitting there all by itself, half filled with bits of garbage and old boxes. I thought I had seen it before.

"Is it the tub from my parents' bathroom?" I asked Wojtasik.

He nodded. "It was so big that we could not move it away further. It is no use to us here. We have built eight outhouses close to the old kitchen entrance."

I looked at the homeless bathtub and noticed, way above near the ceiling, a dusty stag's head staring at me with its sadly resigned glass-made eyes. He too looked very familiar.

The plywood partitions blocked off the vastness of the hall. I followed Wojtasik up the spiral staircase and almost fell on my nose in the darkness. I reached for the familiar light switch, but there were no lamps any more—only the sockets were left.

"We blocked off the window in the hall. This made the staircase very dark," said Wojtasik. "But we can't get any bulbs anywhere. They are terribly scarce."

"I shall have to send you some," I said loudly. I was beginning to feel very strange.

My room looked cluttered but clean. The Wojtasiks slept, ate, cooked, washed, cleaned vegetables and sorted out bags of chemical fertilizers in it. The walls were painted dark brown, but in one spot, over the stove where the paint was chipped off, bits of the old green and pink wallpaper peeked out shyly.

Another family with two children occupied the sitting room next door. I recognized a French commode in the corner, with the brass handles torn off. It came from my mother's bedroom downstairs. Four iron beds filled the room. A wooden washstand with a chipped enamel bowl on it stood between the two windows. Children's clothing and diapers were stacked on a chair next to a primitive gas stove.

"What happened to *your* house?" I asked Wojtasik. He

had had a nice, four-room house with a large garden of his own that Father built for him in the village. We used to stop and confer with him frequently on our way back from church on Sundays. "You were far more comfortable in the old days."

"Yes," he said, "it all happened when the collective was set up. They told us to move into the manor and take over. It seemed like a good prospect to some, but then it became too crowded. In the meantime an official from Kalisz took over my house. You had to be in the Party to live in more than one room. When the collective was disbanded, I was in bed sick, so others moved in there after the *kolkhoz* official was chased out. With the shortage of rooms, I shall never get it again for myself."

We heard hurrying footsteps come up the staircase on the left, and Irka, my former maid, burst into the room. I recognized her immediately because of her very round face and bulging blue eyes. "Oh, Lord," she cried, "what a surprise! And to think we talked about you only the other day! We have read in the papers that many Americans were coming, and we thought that perhaps you would come and see us someday."

She was sobbing and I, too, had tears in my eyes. We hugged each other and walked down to the other side of the house. "Don't look," said Irka. "It's terrible—oh, what a mess it all is!"

A row of ramshackle outhouses stretched where the Maréchal Niel roses used to grow. The smell was very unpleasant. The grounds on the south side of the house were plowed under; it was hard to tell where the paths used to be, but the rare heliotrope bushes were still there; they had grown and spread wide in a cloud of pale-lilac bloom.

Here on the south side of the house the evening was still and remote. Majestic oaks and lime trees protected the house

on both sides. There was a chatter of birds, and a faint low-
ing of cattle could be heard in the distance.

I walked up the steps of the verandah and reached for the
door to the living room. I felt a hand on my shoulder.

"You can't go in," said Wojtasik. He was gentle but firm.
"People are living in there. There are two families in that
room."

I withdrew—as if I had been caught trespassing.

We went back to the front of the house and sat down on
the grass with the others. Yanka, the coachman's daughter,
had arrived, and she proceeded to fill me in on details. It
seems that after Gomulka's speech in October the collective
was spontaneously disbanded.

"It had never worked anyway," put in a young man I
didn't know. "There were too many disputes—too much
haggling. We all hated it, but we were helpless."

Now they each owned between fourteen and twenty-five
hectares of land, depending on the amount of work they put
into the defunct collective. The rest, together with orchards,
was still owned by the State, but now they could buy it, if
they wished. They could own up to one hundred hectares a
person—better than farmers near Warsaw, where the maxi-
mum allowed was fifty.

"For the first time in my life, I really have something to
work for," said Yanka's husband, a tall, husky man with large
hands. "I can pass it on to our children. We are short of
machines and of horses—everyone wanted a horse when we
disbanded. Oh, the battles that went on! It was terrible."

An old man with a drooping mustache came down the
alley of pink chestnuts. He was Nowak, the foreman. He was
born in the village, as were his father and grandfather. Nowak had been foreman at the farm for the last forty-five
years. I shook his hand with delight.

After we had greeted each other and laughed and exchanged family news for a while, I said: "The crops look pretty good, driving here, particularly the barley and the oats. How does the production per *morga* (Polish land measure—about 1.38 acre) compare with my father's day?"

"We don't have enough fertilizers," he said. "And machines—it is lower than it was in your father's day, but this was to be expected. People are learning. This will be the first year that they are on their own, and it should get steadily better from now on. They now have a powerful incentive to work for."

"The collective was not much of a success, I gather. What did you think of it, Nowak?"

"The people hated it. Their work output was zero. At least, in your father's day, they were handsomely paid for their work. They had bonuses and *dozynki* (harvest festivals) and plenty to eat. They worked as their grandfathers had—for your people. The *kolkhoz* was nominally theirs, but, in fact, nobody owned anything. They resented it when I rang the farm bell in the old days to announce the day's work, but they hated the *kolkhoz* bell even more. Now they are on their own. We shall see."

"What land do you own, Nowak?" I inquired.

"Oh, I took that parcel near Marysin—you know, where *Yasniepan* (the brightly illuminated sir), your father, used to experiment with hybrid wheats. I know that soil and subsoil; I hope to buy the adjoining ten hectares."

"Good luck to you, Nowak. I hope you do. It will be a nice bit to leave to your children later on. I remember Marysin very well. Are the cherry trees that you planted along the road to Sulislaw still there?"

Nowak was famous for his green thumb. Each time Mother planned a new avenue of trees she asked Nowak to supervise the planting.

It was strange sitting out there on the lawn among people

I had known all my life, talking about things that we owned
and they took without compensation. There was no bitterness between us. They liked me because they had loved and
respected my parents in the past. To them, I was *their Yasna
panienka*. They had watched me learn to walk and ride
horses. We had shared many Christmases together and danced
at the harvest festival each year when the crops were in. Ever
since I was ten I had been godmother at christenings of their
children, and there were innumerable Christines in the village
whose namedays fell on the same date as mine. Had the place
still remained a collective, we would probably all have shared
the same sorrow. Now they were on their own. For the first
time in generations, they were independent landowners. I
wished them all the luck in the world, but I could not look
at the house without feeling angry and sad. The family crest
was still there, high above on its tablet of stone. Under it was
a long line of washing floating out from a dilapidated window frame.

"Yes, I know it is sad," Yanka said, putting a comforting
hand on my knee. "We had hoped they would make it into a
swietlica (lecture hall), as they have done in some places, but
now too many people have moved in. But, you know, we all
look after the chapel, and the priest comes from Kalisz each
Sunday, as before. Let's walk there. We will show you."

We walked down the long alley of chestnuts, just as I
had done hundreds of times in my childhood, followed by
Nowak and the others. The chapel indeed looked untouched.
It was clean and well kept; the crimson pillows in our pew
had faded but only slightly. The sun streamed through the
tall windows and played shadows on the stone walls outside.
We knelt down, and all prayed silently. I was putting my
memories to rest.

After that, we all walked around for a while. They demanded to see pictures of my daughter and my husband—

and of the "New York skyscrapers, if possible." They told
me I looked pretty but "too thin," and asked me to write to
them from New York. We talked of the tragic death of my
brother, and of my sister's marriage in Belgium and her three
children. They had had news of my mother and were glad
she was soon coming to the States to see us. (As I write, she
is now here in New York.) I felt that they were relieved,
once they sensed that I did not plan to reproach them for
stripping me of my rightful possessions.

Their attitude toward me had changed, as compared with
the old days. The old people still bowed low, kissed my hand
and called me *"Yasna panienka."* The younger ones were
friendly, but they felt that they were my equals and they
wanted me to know it. We shook hands, discussed the crops
and Gomulka, talked about the young people who had gone
away from the farm and who were now coming back rapidly.
Irka, the maid, had two brothers studying for an engineering
degree. One of the foreman's five sons was a director in a
coal mine in Silesia. This was new—it was progress. In the old
days, Irka's brother would probably have remained a farm
laborer, or perhaps he could have become a butler or a coachman at our place—if he happened to be presentable. I was
glad for them and I said so. We indeed were many bends
down the river from the days of my pony rides in this park.

The sun was low when I came back from the stables, which
now housed cows and farm horses. The call of the cuckoo
was heard from over the distant fields. "One, two, three,
four," counted Irka. "How many years to my wedding day,
tell me, cuckoo." She turned to me smiling. "Do you remember the plans that had been laid out for years for your and
your sister's weddings?" she asked. "I always regret that the
war came before your wedding took place. The bottles in
the cellar . . . Teodor and I used to count them and wonder."

I, too, remembered the long rows of bottles in the cellars,

labeled: "For Krysias' wedding," "For Zosia's wedding."
Wines of all sorts, liqueurs, and champagne, many put away
on the day we were born: there was enough to entertain one
hundred people and more.

"What happened to our wine cellars?" I asked. "Are they
empty?"

"The Germans took care of them during the occupation,"
said Irka. "We store potatoes in them now."

Kaziulek, the coachman, came running to where I was
standing with Irka. He was dressed in his black Sunday suit
and looked scrubbed and unchanged from before. He threw
his cap on the ground and bent down to my knees, just as he
used to greet my mother in days past. I tried to shake hands
with him, but he was wiping tears with the rough material of
his sleeve. "I could not believe it," he said, "when Yanka told
me you were here. I had to go home and clean up. You have
always seen me in uniform. You remember how those livery
buttons were shined? So I am the last to arrive. We have no
transportation these days—just our feet."

Kaziulek never walked anywhere, any time. He always had
a pair of horses to drive. "I still see you," he said, looking in
the direction of the lake, "you and Master Ian, the day you
fell into that pond with the goats. How you were frightened
and wet! I told you to stick to the ponies from then on."

It was an episode from the early days of my childhood.
Ian, my brother, and I were given a pair of white goats.
Someone told us they worked well in a harness. We had a
fancy red harness made in Kalisz, put the white goats in it behind a little four-wheel cart, armed ourselves with a whip
and drove off in the direction of the pond. The goats had
plenty of pep and proved to be far stronger than we were.
We found ourselves and the cart upside down in the pond
and were rescued from drowning by Kaziulek.

". . . and that day at the flower show," Kaziulek kept talking volubly, "do you remember when a sudden crack of the whip frightened the four-in-hand you were driving? You almost let the reins go!"

It seemed like the past century to me, but to him the memory was quite recent.

It was time to go back. We had more than five hours' drive back to Warsaw. Ed and Terry Symans appeared from the adjoining woods with a full basket of mushrooms. We walked back toward the green car, which was entirely surrounded by a crowd of enraptured onlookers. I said good-bye to Irka and to Yanka, and to Nowak, the foreman, and to Kaziulek, who stood leaning against the split trunk of an acacia tree. "I am thinking of *Yasniepan*, your father," he said. "He and I were the same age, except that I was born in November. God bless his memory; we often talk about him, you know."

I looked for Wojtasik, the gardener, and saw him hurrying up to the terrace with a huge armful of jasmin. "These are the only flowers I could find," he said, with a rueful expression. "All of your flowering bushes have gone. Take these—it will remind you of your house—and good luck."

I got into the car and we left. The scent of jasmin stayed with me for many days.

CHAPTER 7

The Ancient Hymn

THE little white country church near Lowicz was packed solid with people. They overflowed through the doorways into the little garden beyond. Around them stretched a shimmering expanse of ripening wheat.

They were mostly young people—men and women between twenty and forty-five years of age—local peasants, farmers in their black Sunday clothes, factory workers, merchants from the neighboring town and large numbers of children. Many carried multi-colored banners with appeals to the Virgin Mary embroidered in gold and silvery thread: "Holy Mary, Mother of God, protect us; do not abandon us, we are your children." They were intense in their concentration; they had come here to get comfort, to gather strength from the ritual of the Mass and from the act of communal worship.

The young farmer standing next to me, brown and robust like a healthy tree trunk, was praying with eyes half closed: "May Jesus be praised forever and ever." With bowed head he kneeled down as the Eucharist was being raised.

Each Sunday throughout Poland, the churches are overflowing. It is an inspiring spectacle. Churches of Roman and Gothic style, Renaissance and baroque, great cathedrals with spires and simple small country churches, many rebuilt since the war—all are bursting with people. Thousands of shrines line country lanes and road crossings. Local people trudge through the mud and the snow, lovingly decorating them with twining boughs and paper flowers.

The holiest shrine of all, the citadel of Polish faith, is Jasna Gora, the Shining Mountain, the Pauline monastery at Czestochowa.

A wide avenue of birches leads up from the industrial town of Czestochowa to the summit of a commanding hill, which dominates the rolling countryside for miles. A towering church, surrounded by a fortress, walled in by medieval ramparts, surges toward the sky. The basilica, the cloisters, the bastioned walls have an exhilarating lightness and harmony, in spite of the agglomeration of styles and different architectural periods. Successive generations of Pauline monks have modified and adopted them according to the style of the day. The chapel of Jasna Gora houses the miraculous image of the Black Madonna, Poland's most treasured ikon. The picture is said to have been painted by Saint Luke, the Apostle, on a table of dark cypress wood built by Saint Joseph; the Holy Virgin sat in front of Saint Luke while he painted—says the legend. The picture was rescued from the ruins of Jerusalem in the year 70 A.D., brought to Byzantium, presented to Charlemagne by the Byzantine Emperor Nicephorus. In the 14th century a German prince presented it to the Polish King Casimir, who left it with the Pauline monks at Jasna Gora for safekeeping. Some hundred years later, brigands tried to steal the picture and carry it across the border into Germany, but when they arrived at the border their horses, "moved by a miraculous force," refused to go any further. The picture had to be returned to the monastery.

The real "miracle of Jasna Gora" took place 301 years ago, when more than ten thousand Swedish troops besieged the monastery's bastioned walls throughout a long, bitter winter.

The monks, under the command of the heroic Abbot Kordecki, assisted by a handful of Polish troops, held out against the besieging forces. The "Swedish deluge," as historians refer to it, swept over the entire country; Czestochowa remained one of the few unconquered cities and strongholds in Poland. After all his attacks had been successfully hurled back by the monks, General Miller, the Swedish commander, ordered that the siege be lifted. He had a near-mutiny on his hands, as his soldiers refused to go on fighting; they swore that "their own bullets came back at them bouncing from the monastery walls," and that "heavenly forces were on the side of the monks," whose ammunition was supposed to have run out weeks before. The soldiers said they could clearly see the figure of a lady in a blue cloak, floating above the basilica spires and covering the fortress with her mantle.

The defense of the monastery turned the war in Poland's favor. It revived the weakened morale of the nation and restored its willingness to fight. Swedish troops were driven out of the country. King Jan-Kazimierz, King of Poland and Grand Duke of Lithuania, declaring that "here was a clear case of miraculous intervention by the Virgin," pledged himself and his nation to the service of "Our Lady, Queen of the Crown of Poland."

To this day Polish Catholics annually renew their vows to her. In 1957 Stefan Cardinal Wyszynski, the Primate of Poland, led the nation in renewing the pledge. It was also the opening of a novena of nine Marian years, which will culminate in the thousandth anniversary of Poland's conversion to Christianity, which took place in 966 A.D.

The summit of the hill has been leveled to provide an immense wide-open space, perhaps twice the size of the Piazza di San Pietro in Rome. It was late afternoon and the expanse was filled by a sea of humanity. There must have been hundreds of thousands of them; over a million it was later reported. They stood there quietly; some prayed, some gazed upward at the ramparts covered with Polish national flags, on which a temporary altar had been erected. Many fingered rosary beads or knelt at the Stations of the Cross. They had come from all over Poland: mountaineers from the Tatras, wearing their richly embroidered felt capes; little farmers' wives from near Lowicz, in green and yellow striped costumes; the Mazovian fishermen's wives from Kurpie, in striped shawls; workers, farmers in everyday clothes—a vast concourse of pilgrims—some of whom had journeyed here on foot to pay homage to the Virgin Mary, Queen of Poland. It was the hour of the procession of the Eucharist, after which Cardinal Wyszynski was to preach.

The long procession came out of the basilica, slowly winding its way along the battlements. Here they came: the clergy in their magnificent vestments, the solemn choir boys in bright red surplices, carrying tall, white candles, the bejeweled mitres of the bishops, the scarlet robes of the cardinals. Banner after banner, choir after choir, the full rich panoply of the liturgical pomp of the Catholic Church unfolded majestically along the medieval ramparts.

We all sank to our knees as "Venite Adoremus" was played and the gold monstrance, resplendent with jewels, was raised above the altar, high against the darkening sky. The entire multitude prayed in silence, while the long shadows of the evening played upon the sharpness of the hill.

Suddenly there was a hush, the moment everyone had been waiting for. Stefan Cardinal Wyszynski appeared in the little chapel above the priory and prepared to lead the congregation in the oath to the Virgin Mary. There was a sudden craning of necks, a silent pressure forward as if not to miss a single word he might say. One could sense the adoration of the vast, human mass, pressed shoulder to shoulder, and the love they felt for the commanding figure of the man, whom they regard as the saviour of their country. The Cardinal told the story of Poland's dedication to the Virgin Mary by Jan Kazimierz 301 years ago. The years have seen many changes in Poland's fortunes—moments of disaster, ruin and revival; an occasional moment of triumph. Now was the time to renew the dedication—the danger to Poland had never been greater.

In a vibrant, masculine voice the Cardinal repeated the oath: "Queen of Poland, I renew the pledges of our fathers and know thee as our Patroness and Queen. I promise Thee to do all that lies in my power that Poland may in truth be the Kingdom of Thy Son and Thine. I promise to live without mortal sin; I promise to be faithful to the Holy Church and its pastors. I promise to defend every child conceived; I promise to keep marital faith and to guard the unity of my family. I promise to live peacefully, to forgive all wrongs and to do good to everyone; I promise to begin a relentless struggle with my faults and bad habits and to follow in the path of virtues. I promise to spread honor and devotion to Thee in my surroundings and throughout the Polish land."

"We swear to Thee, Mary, Queen of Poland, we swear to Thee," the crowd joined the response, their eyes upon the bulky outline of the fortress above them.

I looked at the human sea around me. This was an extraordinary crowd; nearly every face bore a history of suffering. It was the face of a nation that had been cruelly tried and which in its hour of need was turning to the Holy Mother for strength.

The woman next to me was lost in a fervent prayer; we had come here together, and I knew her history. She was not old; she could not have been more than forty, but she looked much older. Her eyes were of a profound Slavic blue and there were deep lines on her face. This woman in the last eighteen years had suffered more than any Westerner could imagine. She had lived under the German occupation, had spent one and a half years in forced labor, watched her six-year-old son die, because no drugs against pneumonia were available. Later, when the Russians came, her husband was sent to prison, and she had to work long hours to feed her other two children. There was no one to help her, as most of her friends and relatives were under similar stress. She had had far less of anything, of personal possessions, of security and of care than women in most other countries. But she had strength. She could face suffering and political persecution and always come out on top. She also had serenity, which came to her from her faith.

Cardinal Wyszynski raised his hand in blessing. A monk stationed near the temporary altar gave a signal and suddenly the mass of humanity burst into Poland's ancient hymn:

"God, who for centuries, has given Poland both Glory and Might;
Who has preserved Her with Your sacred shield
From enemies always ready to engulf Her,
To Your altars, Oh God, we bring our fervent prayers,
Preserve the independence of our country forever and ever."

The powerful song, which until recently had been banned, surged toward the evening sky, toward the spires of the basilica and the bastions on which flickering lights had appeared. The sea of people swayed gently, moved by one common emotion. The women in the crowd were crying—and so was I.

The churches of Poland are full. The country has a Communist government, but its people worship their God with ardent faith. Three-quarters of the congregations are young people, men and women, whose religious convictions Communism had hoped to invade in the last twelve years of its reign. Among the churchgoers are numerous Communist Party members.

How can a Catholic be a Communist? He can't. The two ideologies mutually exclude each other. The disciples of Lenin do not admit the existence of God.

Poland is 96 percent Catholic, but the man at its helm is an atheist. Out of a population of 28 million, probably less than 500,000 are regular Communist Party members. Many of the alleged Communists go to Mass, marry in religious ceremonies, send their children to be baptized in a church.

The answer to this strange paradox lies in Poland's thousand years of history during which Catholicism has been so deeply woven into the fabric of national life that it is impossible for a Pole to get away from it. The Poles are a sentimental people and deeply attached to tradition. Christianity came to Poland from Rome (unlike the other Slav nations, Yugoslavia, Russia, Bulgaria); it has become an intrinsic part of the heritage of Western culture to which all Poles are proud to belong.

A young Communist Party member wants to marry a girl he has known for some years and is deeply in love with. Her parents will object to the marriage on the grounds that he is a Communist. The girl herself, though in love, would not dream of being married without the blessing of her church. So what is the young man to do? He gives in and asks only that it all be done with discretion. Their children will naturally be baptized; they will be taught religion in the schools. How else? Everyone else's children are. With years the one-time Communist will be seen in church frequently. He may still belong to the Party—"his second face," as some of them refer to it jokingly—but it will be an allegiance in name only. It happens occasionally that the wife loses her faith and that she drifts away from the Church after marriage, but such cases are comparatively few. Poland is an unusually homogeneous country—the pull of daily tradition and of the centuries-old customs weighs heavily on the side of the Church.

A Communist would not find it easy to ignore a religious holiday like Christmas, Easter, Assumption Day, Pentecost or the like. Although he may not go to church, it would be difficult for him to abstain from joining friends during the traditional Christmas meal at a table with the Nativity scene in the center and hay under the tablecloth (to commemorate the Child born in the Bethlehem stable). He and his godless colleagues would be pathetically isolated from the masses in whose service he has supposedly been enrolled.

But tradition is just one of the explanations. A prominent Polish novelist explained it to me this way: "In the last eighteen years, the average person in Poland has had more than an individual's normal share of suffering. They have seen death and danger at close range. No matter how convincing a materialistic doctrine may be"—this man, once a leading Communist intellectual, explained—"when death stares you in the face, there comes to any individual a moment of naked truth, like a sudden illumination. Then the inevitable question arises: *'What is the sense of it all?'* At such a moment the materialistic doctrine, with its purely mathematical structure, will usually fall apart. The man will reach for a crucifix and remember the prayer that his mother used to tell him in his childhood. I know," he said. "I have gone through all this and have seen many of my colleagues do the same.

"The Russians know it only too well. During the war with the Germans, old ikons had to be taken out of dust storage and Orthodox priests were freed from jail to appeal to the religious feelings of the soldiers, whose morale was rapidly faltering. The Polish people have suffered a lot. They have found in religion an inexhaustible source of strength. That's why Communism has lost its battle with the church and has capitulated all the way."

Out in the countryside near Lublin I was told of the following conversation:

"Why is it, Father, that when you ring the bells for service all the villagers come running, but when I call a Party meeting, hardly anyone shows up?" asked the young Party secretary in a village, while talking to the local priest. "What is your secret?"

"Easy enough," answered the priest. "You and I both promise the people paradise, but you have already given them a taste of yours."

An old-time Communist and nihilist said to me: "In the days of our battle with the Church we sometimes asked ourselves, 'How did the Apostles manage to capture human hearts so readily?' The answer came to a Party official one evening, when he happened to tune in on the Sermon on the Mount on the radio. It was a BBC Sunday broadcast from London. He listened to it for a while, then banged his fist on the table with despair: '*They* really knew how to make propaganda; they were masters at it; who are we by comparison?' "

The anti-Church campaign waged by the Stalinists in Poland failed because of the intensive nationalism of the Poles and also because the Church of Rome has always been stronger in Poland than in any other of the satellite countries. The attack turned even lukewarm Catholics into devout churchgoers; to many people the Church became a symbol of resistance against the system.

In October, 1956, Stefan Cardinal Wyszynski was released from prison by Gomulka. He demanded that teaching of religion be reinstated in schools. (Later 94 percent of the parents asked that their children be given religious instruction.) He asked for immediate resumption of religious publications, liberty of religion in hospitals, Army posts, factories, universities, etc. He demanded that all imprisoned bishops, monks and priests be released forthwith. All his demands were granted. Gomulka needed him badly. The country's anti-Red fever, fanned by the October events, was mounting. Hungary had just exploded. It seemed that nothing short of the Cardinal's tremendous personal authority could control the nation's headlong rush to freedom, which in the circumstances could only result in the horror of Soviet armed intervention.

History has no precedent for the strange partnership that governs today's Poland. The old-time Communist and the saintly Cardinal are the only two leaders that the Poles trust. In spite of the ideological gulf that separates them, they have two things in common: a deep genuine love of Poland and a thorough distrust of Russia. They also have both been imprisoned, which is always an asset in the eyes of the Poles, who have a fondness for martyrs. Their partnership is close and they lean on each other in difficult political moments. Their goal is identical: to keep Poland's precarious semi-independence alive.

This strange alliance of the Catholic Church and Communism is working smoothly. The Catholic masses, including some of the most ardent anti-Communists, have placed themselves wholeheartedly behind Gomulka because they see in him the only hope of escaping another Russian bondage. The Communists, on the other hand, recognizing the enduring power of the Church, admit that they have failed miserably in their struggle against it.

The Cardinal believes, with Gomulka, that any attempt to abandon lip service to Communism would invite Russian intervention. Like the majority of the Poles, he believes that Gomulka's administration must be actively supported in order to save the country from physical disintegration. It is in the light of these considerations that he took the unprecedented step of appealing to the country to vote for the Communist candidates during the January election. On January 20 the world saw the extraordinary spectacle of Polish country priests in their vestments leading their parishioners to the polling places to vote for a Communist leader, an atheist whose soul has surely long been possessed by the devil.

Compromise? Perhaps—but always in the name of the age-long political wisdom.

The Catholic support for the regime does not imply any weakening in the struggle the Church wages against the obnoxious doctrine. It is simply a modus vivendi, an uneasy alliance formed under unprecedented political circumstances. Its object is national survival, and to this aim, unity is of supreme importance.

Warsaw newspaper wags tell of the following conversation:

"I am going to Moscow next week," says Gomulka to Cardinal Wyszynski. "Don't you excommunicate me; it will ruin my prestige with the people."

"I am going to Rome in a few days," answered the Cardinal. "Don't you dare to put any of my bishops in jail."

The story sums up the relationship pretty clearly.

In dealing with the government the Cardinal got all he asked for. His parish is stronger today than it has been for years, and it is bound closely to Rome. The Stalinists once tried to create a national Polish church, but their efforts ended in a resounding fiasco. So far, the government has fulfilled its part of the bargain. The Church has no complaints— as of now, though the future is anyone's guess.

In prewar Poland, the Catholic Church was criticized by some for being "reactionary"—closer to the upper stratas of society than to the roots of the country. No one would say this today. In the classless society of today's Poland the clergy is one with the masses of peasantry and working people. Like the majority of the country, it desires no return to the prewar system of large landowners and industrial cartels; it has, in a modified way, accepted the main economic tenets of Polish socialism such as distribution of landholdings, State-ownership of the main sources of production, central planning.

Gomulka and his Party, on the other hand, will tolerate the existence of numerous Catholic organizations so long as they content themselves with publishing newspapers and so long as they concentrate on the propagation of the faith. What they will not tolerate is the emergence of a Catholic Party—such as existed before the war—as a political force with its own lists of candidates for elections, which would set itself in direct competition to the Communist Party. It would be easy for the Catholics to achieve such a parliamentary majority, but the consequences would be disastrous for the Church. Wyszynski knows it; he keeps scrupulously out of politics and, on his orders, so does the clergy. The January election was the only exception that was made; it followed a direct request from Gomulka. It is the consensus of many observers that the prospects for peace between the Church and the Communist Party in Poland seem good—at least for the time being.

At the time of Wyszynski's visit to Rome, Pope Pius XII approved the Cardinal's actions. He gave him his complete blessing.

The chancelleries of the Vatican examine political problems of their day from the perspective "what will it do to the Church a hundred or more years from now?" They can afford to be pliable.

I shall never forget the first time I met Stefan Cardinal Wyszynski, a few weeks after my arrival in Poland.

It was the beginning of March, and the early spring sun

shone brightly over the generous expanse of newly rebuilt Miodowa Street. There was snow on the ground and on the sloping roofs of the houses, and it lay in wide patches in gardens, behind the high brick walls on both sides of the street. I walked past the graceful façade of the Ministry of Agriculture and turned left into the rectangular courtyard of Miodowa 17, the three-story, yellow-tinged palace of the Primates of Poland. The vast entrance hall was crowded with clergy, nuns and numerous lay visitors. I found the pleasant, round-faced chaplain Padacz, standing at the foot of the winding stairway.

"His Eminence will see you in a few moments," he said, and led me to a small, sunny room with a very high ceiling, red velvet armchairs and a large window overlooking the snow-covered walks of a formal Italian garden. My watch said five minutes before noon.

A few days before, I had asked a Communist deputy: "Who, next to Gomulka, is the most powerful man in Poland?" I was thinking of one in the Communist hierarchy.

"It is Stefan Cardinal Wyszynski, of course!" he said without hesitation. "He knows it and we all know it. Sometimes I think that he is the stronger of the two."

Now I thought of the history of the man I was about to talk to and of the road that led him to the pinnacle he is occupying today.

He had been born poor in the little village of Zuzela, near Bialystok, on the river Bug, in what used to be Central Poland but is now close to the new Russian border. He was one of five children of the village organist and school teacher. His mother died when he was nine years old and his father married again. The boy attended the local parochial schools and later went to Warsaw High School. At eighteen he decided to become a priest. His intelligence and energy drew the attention of his superiors and he was sent to the University of Lublin, where he won a doctorate in canon law and social sciences. He then spent several years traveling in Italy, France, Germany and Belgium, and became known as an authority on social and labor problems. He wrote several books on unemployment, the rights of labor and a popular brochure on Catholicism and trade unions. In 1939, when the Germans occupied Poland, the 38-year-old Father Wyszynski was assigned to underground work in Warsaw. He worked hard, with devotion, mostly among workers and students. In 1946 he became Bishop of Lublin. He chose as his motto the Latin phrase, "Soli Deo" (I serve God alone). On January 3, 1949, just as the Communists were beginning to bring pressure on the Polish youth, Cardinal Sapieha—the distinguished and fearless Archbishop of Krakow—brought him the Vatican nomination for Primate of Poland. He had never wanted to be a diplomat, even less a politician, but as the Communist pressure on the Church steadily mounted, he was soon to learn the necessity of being both.

Priests were being arrested throughout the country, dragged off to prison in their vestments. Lands held by religious orders were confiscated. The Catholic clergy's welfare organization, "Caritas," with its large money reserves, was handed over to a Russian-supported organization headed by a renegade Pole, who had once worked for the Gestapo.

Wyszynski tried to find a modus vivendi by negotiating an agreement with the Stalinists, but they promptly proceeded to break it. They fired priests from their posts as religious teachers, abolished existing Church publications and began a methodical persecution of the religious orders.

On June 4, 1953, the Cardinal warned Polish Catholics to prepare themselves for martyrdom. A full-scale battle between the Church and the Communist Government was drawing near.

On the evening of Friday, September 25, 1953, the Cardinal held his regular evening service in the Church of Saint Anne in Warsaw. He walked the few city blocks to his residence in Miodowa Street. In the gathering he saw his courtyard filled with secret-police people with guns. An armed tank guarded the entrance. His 80-year-old father, two nuns and several visiting priests were ordered to face the wall or be shot.

"The Lord be praised," said the tall, commanding figure to the police intruders.

They raised their guns in reply.

At this moment the Cardinal's Alsatian dog ran out onto the courtyard and, barking ferociously, bit the hand of the soldier nearest to his master. The bite was not serious, but the Cardinal insisted on personally bandaging the soldier's hand.

That night he was taken away to a monastery near Rywold and later to a monastery near Lizbark, in Polish Silesia, the first two of four consecutive places of detention.

A white notice went up on the doors of the Church of the Holy Cross where he was to preach the next day: "The Cardinal will not preach here this morning."

It took the regime three days to break the news to the people.

While in prison, he suffered no physical hardship, but there were microphones in his room and constant police supervision. He spent the days writing, studying history and the works of Lenin and Marx.

"I am better versed in the Communist doctrine than any of the Polish Politburo members," he liked to remark later with a twinkle. "I get the better of them in a discussion any time."

One day in 1955 a delegate from Bierut, the Polish Chief of State, came to see him in prison. "If you agree to give up your post as Primate," he said, "we will set you free. You will be able to preach, say Mass and be with your people."

"I prefer to pray for you here, gentlemen," replied Wyszynski, and he went back to his studies of Marx.

On Friday, October 19, 1956, Gomulka took over in Poland. The following Wednesday two men got into a small, black car and drove the 300 miles from Warsaw to the isolated monastery near Komancza in the foothills of the Carpathian mountains. One of them was Gomulka's friend, Wladyslaw Bienkowski, the newly appointed Minister of Education; the other, Zenon Kliszko, a Communist deputy, Gomulka's ideological adviser. They offered unconditional release. The Cardinal dictated his terms.

On Sunday, October 28, the Cardinal's black 1948 Ford swung into the courtyard of the Primate's Palace which he had left just a little over three years before.

The following Sunday he preached at the Church of the Holy Cross, where he had failed to appear the Sunday after his arrest.

"I am a little late in coming to you," he said, "a little more than three years. Forgive me. This is the first time I have been tardy."

As I was recalling the events, a door at the opposite side of the room opened and a tall, erect figure in scarlet robes came briskly into the room.

"I am glad to see you, my child," said Stefan Cardinal Wyszynski, and I bent down in a curtsey and kissed the holy ring on his hand.

He motioned me to one of the red velvet chairs. His clean-cut features were sharp; his eyes were blue and alive, and I thought that he had the longest fingers of anyone I had ever seen. There was strength in his face but also an extraordinary repose, as if years of inner reflection had given him a serenity that no outside element could break. This man does not struggle any more, I thought, he won the battle with himself long ago. His road lies clear before him and he *knows* that God is with him.

We talked of many things: of the economic conditions in Poland, of the poverty of the clergy and of life in America, where he had never been. We talked of the American loan to Poland and of the U. S. help to Yugoslavia. We discussed Senator Knowland's recent pronouncement and his influence on U. S. politics. We talked of my family in Poland, of my parents, whom he remembered, of several aunts he knew well, and of my marriage to a U. S. Protestant. His answers were quick and direct, and his questions were gentle but searching.

There were many things in our country that to him seemed incomprehensible. Why, for instance, should a great U. S. Senator object to the idea of helping Poland, a country which had shown so much courage, had been so cruelly tried, where poverty is acute and whose people long to reaffirm their ties with the West?

"There is freedom in Poland, freedom of talk and of worship, more than in Yugoslavia; still Yugoslavia received over a billion dollars in American aid, though its Archbishop Stepinac is still in a Communist jail. How can the American people permit it?" he wondered.

He felt that Americans of Polish descent should be encouraged to visit Poland and that they should bring their children along; the rich heritage of Polish history and culture should not be thrown away by default. Circumstances had changed since October—everyone should feel free to come.

He said that he had read of the discussions in the Polish-American press in the United States on whether aid should be extended to Poland.

"If you see your child ill, do you debate whether you should give him help or not?" he asked. "If you see your mother in need, do you wrack your brain and discuss whether it is suitable to hurry with help? Everyone who can should aid those who are in dire need and this nation *is* in dire need."

I sensed the stress he lives under, the constant knotty problems arising from a situation that is as dangerous as it is novel; his deep mistrust of Communism and of its followers, and his concern for the widespread drinking and general loosening of morals in the country—the damage inflicted on the nation by the lawlessness and nihilism of the past epoch.

"Political systems come and go, but the Catholic Church is here to remain; it is the long pull that really counts in the end," he said, gazing away into the distance. "The Church is eternal and no materialistic doctrine is strong enough to destroy it. They have tried hard, but we have emerged stronger than ever before. My life is dedicated to my people; they need me and they trust me; they are my children. That is why I came out of prison and why I preach every day. We are going to survive—and win."

He had good words to say for the way the government is carrying out its part of the Church-State agreement. There is active coöperation between the two on the "fight with corruption, absenteeism and lack of discipline" front. Catholic clergymen and Ministry of Education officials were sitting together just then, jointly revising the Stalin-era school textbooks.

"Bless you, my child," he said, rising and making the sign of the cross over me. "Pray for me, for I need it."

I went out into the sunny street, filled with an overwhelming compassion. This task is too much for one man, I thought. Even this spiritual giant will one day break under the burden —and what then will happen to Poland?

Then I remembered his face as I had seen it a few days previously at the Church of Saint Anne in Warsaw, preaching from the pulpit under the glare of a single electric-light bulb.

"He *is* the saviour of Poland," I thought. "This is his destiny and he will fulfill it to the end. Men like him never break—they only suffer. . . ."

CHAPTER 8

An Attractive Communist

"THE Minister will be here in a moment," said the secretary. "He has just telephoned to say that he will not be more than ten minutes late. He rushed home across the street to have a bite of lunch—the first chance he had to break away since early this morning."

I was sitting in a light-paneled office awaiting Wladyslaw Bienkowski, the Minister of Education: writer, politician, old-time Communist, close friend of Mr. Gomulka, admirer of Cardinal Wyszynski, and one of the architects of the Church-State agreement—a man of many contrasts, great charm and outstanding abilities.

"Have you met an attractive Communist yet?" a friend of mine wrote the other day from New York. I thought that the man I was to see shortly was one.

Ever since my arrival in Poland I had been trying to sort in my mind and classify the peculiar breed of Communists I found all over that country. I knew the regular-type Communist—the convinced, ideological Party worker whose motivation is the conquest of the universe for the Red hammer and sickle, who looks at Russia as the leader and paragon of all virtues. In a non-Communist country such a man will conspire to overthrow the existing government by force.

I have also known the career-type, the most despicable of all, who is a Communist for reasons of expediency and immediate personal gain, the ruthless official and eager-beaver Party man, who will desert to the West the minute the going gets tough.

I knew of the national Communists, like Tito and Mao-tse-tsung of China, who believe in Marx and in Lenin, but refuse to recognize the ideological supremacy of the Kremlin.

Now, in Poland, I had come across something else. I had met Communist Party members who went to Mass and got married in a church, who would discourse for hours on the horror of a police system and swear it had been done away with forever in Poland, who believed in private enterprise, as long as the State owned the basic sources of products. They hated Russia with a cold, blinding passion and would tell me that the welfare of their country far transcended any tenets of the Communist faith.

What was their basic creed, I wondered. As far as I could understand it, they were intent on repairing the social injustices brought about by the former class system, keeping the basic means of production in the hands of the State, so there would be no more large landowners and huge industrial cartels. They proclaimed there should be a certain amount of central planning and control over investment capital to prevent it from going speculative.

"In the present political and geographical position of our country it would take a man of almost superhuman altruism to invest his money in a long-range project, no matter how worthy," Mr. Lipinski, the pleasant, London-educated economist, a deputy chairman of the newly created State Economic Council, had said to me one night at dinner.

I had talked to Woroszylski, the brilliant, young intellectual, editor of the *Nowa Kultura* in Warsaw, who with several others of his group fought in the Hungarian uprising.

To him, freedom of speech and of writing was an unaliena-
ble right; there should be no more censorship. "But," he said,
"it may surprise you if I insist, but I still am a Communist
and I want to remain one."

"You are a sentimentalist and you are attached to a fiction,"
I said to him, with impatience. "You are no more a Communist than I am!"

"We 'revisionists' have always been more flexible than the
conservative Stalinists," he remarked. "But we still like to
think of ourselves as Communists, even after the Hungarian
events."

I admitted that I was getting confused.

To me, the so-called "revisionists"—the liberal wing of the
Communist Party in Poland as opposed to the hard core of
"conservative" Stalinists, always seemed more like the Social
Democrats in their creed. I was sure that most of the leading
Communists in Poland were at least unconsciously the same.
No applied definition of Marxist-Leninism can long exist in
a country where there is complete freedom of speech and
where the machinery of police terror has been as joyously
and as thoroughly dismantled as in Poland. Definitions vary
with geographical boundaries, I decided.

Now I was waiting to see the man to whom the revisionists
since October have been looking as their leader. I had met
him before, and I liked him.

Son of a factory worker in the industrial city of Lodz,
Bienkowski has been a Communist for most of his fifty-one
years. Though he had not traveled much outside Poland, his
way of thinking was essentially Western. He had a direct and
precise way of talking, devoid of the usual Communist dia-
lectics. What I liked best about him was his wonderful sense
of humor: delightfully sharp, sophisticated, going straight to
the point, it was a quality unknown among his top-ranking
colleagues of the "socialist bloc." His formal schooling had

been sketchy and he was mostly self-taught, but he possessed an almost encyclopedic knowledge on a wide range of subjects including history, music, literature, architecture and economics.

"For seven years I worked in the Biblioteka Narodowa (the Polish equivalent of our Library of Congress)," he told me the first time I went to see him. "I would like to return there soon."

He had served the Communist Party as an underground cell organizer at the time of the German occupation, then as a writer of pamphlets and the political brain of the Party. In 1945, when the Communist regime was set up, he became a member of the Central Committee of the Polish Communist Party, then deputy to the Sejm (Parliament) and member of the inner circle of the Party Secretariat. No one will ever know what happened within the inner councils of the Party in those days, but all of a sudden, in 1948, Mr. Bienkowski was denounced as a deviationist, stripped of all political office and sent to the Biblioteka Narodowa to oblivion. With Gomulka's return, Bienkowski came out of oblivion. His blunt articles denouncing the lunacy of the Stalinist rule during the last twelve years in Poland made him a popular figure. And shortly after the October events, Gomulka asked him to take over the all-important Ministry of Education.

Millions of pupils throughout the land had lost confidence in their teachers. They had ceased to believe the truth of what they were officially taught. Children are naturally perceptive and the first to sense a discrepancy between reality and the contents of the familiar textbook. Once the teacher is caught telling a lie, his value as an educator is gone.

Gomulka and Bienkowski realized that even in a Communist system the role of an educator is far different from that of a politician. The educator cannot afford to make vague, diplomatic statements or to leave some questions un-answered. He is forced to supply an explanation that will sat-isfy the inquiring young minds of his pupils. A politician addressing his audience can make all sorts of glib statements without inwardly committing himself—he even can be con-vincing. Not a teacher—the children will detect a false note in the lecture, and their confidence will be gone. It is the same unerring instinct through which they sense fear or joy in an adult—his indifference or his love.

During the last twelve years, Polish teachers had been sub-ject to political control; they had ceased to be educators and had become State employees, transmitting the contents of a textbook according to instructions from above. They became rigid and dogmatic; the gulf between them and their pupils was immense. No wonder that after the October revolution much of the country's resentment turned strongly against the teachers. "*They* are the source of all evil," people said, point-ing at them with their fingers.

To cleanse the atmosphere in the schools, to restore con-fidence in the teacher, to free the educational field from the blight of the Stalinist lie, became one of the most pressing problems of Gomulka's government.

Bienkowski was given the task, and he went at it with en-thusiasm. It was a big job. To begin with, there were no cadres of teachers. During the last twelve years, colleges throughout the country had been training agitators, rather than pedagogues. Vast numbers of older teachers who refused to comply with the method were dismissed or left in disgust. Textbooks had to be revised, following the October-adopted principle that "no more lies shall be told." In the curricular courses, room had to be made for at least four hours of re-ligious teaching a week; priests were put on the payrolls alongside the lay teachers. The general level of studies was depressingly low. The students detested their schools and had learned little or nothing. New incentives had to be devised to make the children work harder.

Bienkowski was doing an outstanding job on these problems. I wanted to ask him not only about the school system but also about many other questions that had puzzled me while traveling throughout Poland. I knew I would get some straight answers.

He came hurrying into the room—a small, wiry man, his freckled face full of cheerfully simulated remorse. "Forgive me for being late," he said warmly, shaking my hand. "I got caught between the annual conference of teachers and the cabinet meeting this morning. I was dead—a tin coffin, nice, light and well-ventilated—what a peaceful spot it would be!"

"You are a long way from it," I said, looking at his tanned, healthy face.

We went into his office, which was light, with mahogany furniture and a fine Oriental rug on the floor.

"How is the school conference progressing?" I asked.

"Oh, it is moving along slowly." He sighed. "There are so many problems. We are now discussing the shortage of adequate school buildings, which is the most important of all. In the Warsaw district alone, 60 percent of all schools are in need of basic repairs. It is the same all over the country, and it is getting worse each year. I have here in front of me a report of the Public Health Commission which states that about 48 percent of all schools lack adequate sanitary facilities."

"I suppose that with the current reduction in the number of ministries and shrinking of the State bureaucratic machinery you were able to pick up some real estate for your purpose?" I inquired.

"We did get some in Warsaw and some in the provinces too. Our best acquisitions so far are the buildings that used to house the former security police. They always had the best of everything." He laughed. "But it is all just a drop in the bucket. Millions of zlotys are needed immediately to build schools all over the country. Unfortunately, this need comes at a time when our entire economy is in grave difficulties. We are desperately trying to cut large outlays down to the bare minimum. In planning for our school system we have to take into account the financial limits of our country; beyond those limits we dare not extend ourselves. Our best hope lies in a direct appeal to the people—to their generosity and to the private initiative of our citizens. After all, the schools are there to serve their most treasured possessions—their children. I have promised to see to it personally that all private effort in this field gets the encouragement it deserves."

"What is your biggest school problem at the moment?" I inquired.

"It is to restore confidence in the teaching profession and the institution of school. You know what the years of Stalinist rule have done to this country. Well, nowhere has the atmosphere of the all-pervading lie taken a heavier toll than in schools. If only the tremendous outlays spent on propaganda and so-called 'political upbringing' had been put into teaching and education, we would be enjoying here today the best school system in the world."

He continued: "We have to clean our school system, just as we have cleansed our political life of the former practice of lying and false statements, of the discrepancy between the theory taught and the practice of everyday life. We have to teach our children the truth. And we have to educate our teachers all over again. Did you know that during the last twelve years close to forty thousand teachers left the profession; some of them willingly, many forcibly removed? Among them were some of the most brilliant pedagogical brains of our country. A few of them have come back, but many will never return. It will take years to repair the wrongs perpetrated during the lunatic period from which we have just emerged."

"How do you reconcile the re-introduction of religious teaching with the tenets of Marxist socialism you are supposed to be building?" I asked.

"This only confirms what I have told you once before, that Poland follows its own road to socialism. This is a Catholic country; with the postwar shift of the frontiers it has become more homogeneous than before: 96 percent of the population is Catholic. The Stalinists have lost their battle with the Church. We have decided to get along with them, and it works. This is the only solution consistent with the freedom we have preached since October. And," he added, with a twinkle in his voice, "it has taken away from religion the magnetism of the forbidden fruit!"

"I shall watch the statistics for the next ten years to see whether what you are thinking about comes true," I said, wondering whether he might have a point there.

The telephone rang, and Bienkowski got up to answer it. It was placed on a little round table at the other end of the room, out of the visitors' hearing. I looked around at the room. As in most of the government offices in Poland, there were no slogans, no enlarged photographs of Lenin or Polish Politburo members on the walls—just a few flower prints, a Polish landscape by an 18th-century Polish painter. That was all; it could have been an American executive's office.

"Mr. Minister," I said, when he came back to the table, "I hear all this talk about the building of socialism in Poland. It sometimes looks like a series of costly experiments, but in the meantime the country is in a desperate economic situation. Don't you think that if all the controls were lifted and private initiative were allowed to operate it might have a salutary effect on the economic picture?"

"No," he replied. "It would only lead to exploitation by the few with money in their pockets. The basis of socialism is that all sources and centers of production belong to the State. The role of private initiative is to fill in the gaps in places where it does not pay the State to take over—such as personal services, laundries, hairdressers, etc.; small enterprises and small-scale tradesmen coöperatives. I would add medium-scale factories and businesses employing up to about forty-five people. Hotels, particularly the larger ones, should belong to the State."

"Oh, Lord," I sighed, "this means that it will always take two hours to get breakfast at the Bristol!"

Bienkowski laughed. "Don't despair. Efficiency will come with greater and more active competition for jobs. It is already starting. Here in Warsaw alone, about thirty thousand people have recently been dismissed from various ministries and agencies run by the State. Someone was telling me recently that there are some excellent State-owned hotels in England."

"They are run by the railroads," I said, "and the English are very efficient by nature."

"You see," he went on, "there are, of course, advantages in the capitalist system; but our people still need the protection of a welfare state. In your world, if an institution does not pay, it means it is no good. Here we look at it differently.

"Take our nursery schools, for example: it costs a working mother 70 zlotys a month to put a child there; he gets three meals a day and good care from 7 A.M. to 6 P.M.—it is a price that any mother is able to afford easily. You will not find it in your country. Of course, you are going to tell me that if the salaries of the husbands were higher, the wives would not have to go to work and leave children in somebody else's care—but still they exist and people are happy to have them.

"Take cultural activities. I saw you at the concert last night. You noticed that most of the audience were working people?

Who attended the concerts before the war in Poland? Only the few who could afford the high price of tickets. Today they are within every workingman's reach, and concert halls are always filled. You have probably been to see *Mazowsze* (a Polish musical based on folk dances—beautifully staged). Such a production would have been impossible before the war; no private person could afford to produce it."

I thought that the economic situation of Poland was such that the State couldn't afford to produce it either.

I asked: "As contacts with the West grow stronger, are you not afraid that the example of our free-wheeling economy will lead you further away from your 'Polish road to socialism'?"

"We *do* want a free exchange of thought and technical information," he repied. "The West is not dangerous to us, because we have *broken off* with the doctrine. We are flexible; we look for solutions emanating from the local needs of our country. We have much to learn, and our people would rather learn from the West than from Russia. But here we have to be careful. Russia is our natural partner. As far as economic exchanges are concerned, we are dependent on the Russians for deliveries of raw materials. Where else could we get ore or cotton without having to pay for it in dollars? Russia holds an economic club over Poland. It is an uncomfortable situation, but there is no remedy for it at the moment."

I remembered the phrase that had been coined last October and that has since become a popular slogan: "Will exchange sovereignty for better geographical position." It summed up the situation of Poland in a nutshell.

We talked about the general political situation for a while, and I asked what he thought about the possibility of a Soviet intervention in Poland.

"I see no such probability on the horizon," he said firmly.

"But a lot will depend on how the current disarmament talks progress and also on the U. S. policy toward China."

He felt that our non-recognition of the "fait accompli" in China was highly unrealistic. "Within our lifetime Russia will matter less to the world than will China. Remember there will be a billion Chinese in twenty years," he said. "Your government insists that they do not exist, but they are multiplying at an amazing rate each day."

"The crucial fact about Poland," he went on, "is that the Party's inner life is no longer totalitarian. My colleagues complain that there is no cohesion, that the Party is falling apart; but this is a small price to pay for inner freedom. With time, we shall achieve unity. Because the process is a free one, it is slow. Only in Poland is the Sejm (Parliament) almost co-sovereign with the Party. You know that it is possible to elect candidates of whom the Party disapproves. Debates are going on all the time, and adverse votes are often cast."

He did not mention that until now Party members took the precaution of always being in a safe majority. But it was my impression that he eagerly supported the divergence of views within the Communist world. Poland was to him at this moment like a schismatic bishopric with a bishop who had lost his faith. What lay at the bottom of the slide? I wondered. Western democracy seemed like a not impossible answer.

I got up to say good-bye. We had been talking for over an hour and I knew there were several people waiting for him outside.

"I have heard you referred to as the Polish Djilas," I said to him laughingly. "Do you think you are likely to end in jail as he has?"

"No, don't worry." He was smiling, but his tone was quite serious. "This is the difference between Poland and Yugoslavia. We have real freedom here now. To fear or not to

fear was the great question in the days of the Stalin regime.
The problem was no less difficult to solve in those days than
it was at one time for the Prince of Denmark. There was an
all-pervading fear; the masses feared Party officials, and officials were afraid of the masses. If an old woman at a market
far in the provinces said something offensive against the government, the whole apparatus of police was immediately put
into action. All this terminated in October. If nothing else
was achieved, we at least won freedom from fear. There will
be no going back.

"I hope to see you again," he said, as I went through the
door. "I shall send you my book on socialism. Who knows?
I may still make a Marxist out of you! I shall try."

"Are you sure *you* are one?" I asked him, in a low voice.
But he only laughed and waved his hand in good-bye.

I went into the Lazienki Park and sat on a bench. "What
a very strange Communist he is," I thought. But I could not
help liking him.

CHAPTER 9

The Krakow Trumpeter

THE countryside began as soon as Warsaw ended. In Poland, there is little suburban shading-off from one to the other. Ten miles outside Warsaw, one might be anywhere. As most of the roads in Poland, this one was straight but very dusty and bumpy. There was hardly any motor traffic on it; sometimes we went for twenty to thirty miles without passing another car.

"I must tell some of the government planners in Warsaw, who seem to be so convinced that their road to socialism will rapidly motorize Poland, that there is far less traffic here now than there was before 1939," I thought.

Though we did not pass many cars, we passed innumerable peasant carts, long and narrow, on which whole big families were riding. This being a Sunday, the women wore gay woolen shawls, while the men were dressed in black clothes and smoked pipes. Whenever we stopped, a crowd of on-lookers collected around our bright-blue 1957 Plymouth station wagon. Children, particularly the boys, climbed on the running board and looked inside at the dashboard with awe.

"Is it all made of plastic?" they asked. "We thought American cars always were! How fast does it run, *Prosze Pan* (please, lady)? Is it 160 kilometers (100 miles), or is it more?

How much gas does it burn? Would one dare to ask for a short ride?"

I loved to look at their faces—the intensely blue eyes that only Slav children possess, the mops of unruly blond hair, the keen, eager expressions and the quick, radiant smiles when allowed to touch a bit of upholstery or the dashboard.

They looked well fed and healthy in spite of their rather poor clothing. They were unafraid and spontaneous, more so than before the war.

"You know," said a Polish friend with whom we were going to Krakow, "I remember when children here used to run away and hide when they saw 'rich' strangers in a car. The classless society of today's Poland has changed them—and it is a change for the better."

We ran out of gas just as we were coming to Kielce, a town halfway between Warsaw and Krakow. It was a Sunday evening, and the one petrol pump in the place was shut tight.

At the market place where we stopped, the usual crowd of little boys gathered round. We asked them to take us to the pump operator's house, determined not to use our emergency supply of five gallons. With three boys squeezed in front with the driver and directing, four in the back beaming and waving to their friends through the window, we went to find Mr. Witek, who lived at the other end of town. When we got there, we were told that he had just left for the movies. Our guides led us to the town's cinema, which was called "Kino Europa," and was showing a prewar German picture starring Erich von Stroheim. Mr. Witek was paged, and he emerged all smiles.

"Oh, what a beautiful car! Is it plastic?" The myth that all American cars are made of plastic has somehow established itself in Poland. Perhaps the reason for it is that plastic is a relatively new material; in backward countries, it is the synonym for the exotic.

We filled the "beautiful plastic car" with gas and proceeded to Krakow, where we arrived late at night.

Most historical places one knows do not live up to their reputation. Krakow is an exception. It is the ancient capital of the Kingdom of Poland, a completely preserved medieval city—the only other like it in Europe is perhaps Nüremberg.

Already in the 13th century, when Warsaw was no more than a village, Krakow was a thriving metropolis and the center of trade between Byzantium and Rome. Here, with their wares to sell, came the Tartar merchants from the Eastern steppes, the Bulgarians and the Turks, and prosperous German and Dutch tradesmen from the cities of the Hanseatic League. Krakow was the great international gathering place between the East and the West. The age was one of monarchy whose frontiers reached far into the East and whose prestige was enormously enhanced by the apparatus of Western civilization, which came to Poland with Christianity from Rome.

The Royal Castle of Wawel, high on a hill above the Vistula, dominates the medieval panorama of Krakow. It was entirely rebuilt at the beginning of the 16th century by the Florentine artist, Franciscus Italus. It has a famous, great courtyard and a crypt where Polish kings lie entombed in massive marble. The great court, with its arches, arcades and galleries, is in a style neither Western nor Eastern, but somewhere between the two. Renaissance and Gothic elements are quite deliberately mixed here, because the Italian architects liked to utilize the skill of the native stonecutters, well versed in the intricate geometrical and floral ornamentation of late Gothic.

In the very center of town rise the two Gothic towers of the Church of Our Lady Mary. The higher of the two is known as the Tower of the Krakow Trumpeter. From a window high up in the tower, overlooking the market square, he plays a brief tune called "The Heynal," and each time, toward the end, he breaks off the song in the middle of the note, as if someone at that moment had taken the trumpet from his lips. This is in memory of a young boy trumpeter who in the year 1241 sounded the Heynal in alarm when Tartars began burning the city. An arrow pierced his throat when he was near the end of his song. That is why the last note begins strongly, trembles and then ceases—broken like the young life of the medieval trumpeter.

The custom has lasted down the centuries. Even during the German occupation and the Russian oppression the trumpet sounded every hour of the day and night. I was thrilled to hear it again.

We drove to the old Francuski Hotel, now renamed The Orbis, and went to bed before the trumpeter sounded midnight. (Two men in the city's fire brigade are regularly assigned to the task of sounding the Heynal, we were told.)

I got up early the next morning and went to call on Karol Estreicher, the curator of the National Museum of Krakow, an old family friend. "Karolek" was in London during the war, but returned to Krakow early in 1945. "I just can't live anywhere else in the world," he said to me before leaving London. "I am a child of Krakow and am going back to the Museum and to the Jagiellonska Library, where I belong." For the last four generations, the Estreichers have been professors of history and art at the University of Krakow. They were part of the city.

I found him standing in the courtyard of the Jagiellonska Library, next to the brooding stone statue of Copernicus, directing the renovation work on an arcade. He wore an old windbreaker and a tattered pair of brown corduroy trousers. His black, tousled hair was as unruly as ever. He radiated energy and good humor.

"I fell off my chair when I received your post card from Warsaw," he said, giving me a big hug. "I had lost track of you completely and did not even know your married name. What fun to see you reappear like this after twelve years!"

We walked down narrow Saint Anne Street to the corner where Jagiellonska meets the Street of the Pigeons and sat down on a bench under an elm tree. He told me about his life since the war, all of which was centered around Krakow and the museums; about the long search for Polish national treasures in the postwar years, which were scattered throughout Germany as a result of the occupation, about the miraculous recovery of the Altar of Wit Stwosz, a famous masterpiece of medieval sculpture in wood, which he had found in a German castle in Bavaria. We talked about the project of a modern extension to the Jagiellonska Library and about the book he was writing. It was going to be a novel, he said, half history and half fiction, and it was going to be finished before Christmas.

The great excitement in his life at the moment was the news that finally, after many years, he would be allowed to have a house built for himself and live in it with his family without having to share it with others.

"For years we have been sharing a kitchen and an antiquated bathroom with four other families in the building," he told me. "Now, finally, we shall be on our own. Restrictions on private building have been lifted so long as it is just a one-family house. You should see the activity that has suddenly spurted up in this town! It's fantastic."

We walked over to the university buildings. This university was more than 100 years old when Columbus discovered America.

I looked at the crowd of young people who were milling around in the pale sunshine, wearing corduroy slacks and sweaters. They looked very much as students do everywhere in the world. It was hard to guess that their cares had to do with eating on twenty cents a day, washing their own clothes, finding an odd stove for their unheated dormitories or a job to pay for books. These were the same boys and girls who last October stood disciplined and ready to fight the Soviet Army.

"Karolek," I asked, "what do your students think? Do they want to remain home and rough it, or do they want to go abroad and stay there?"

"They do not want to leave Poland," he answered, "but they would love to go abroad for short trips. They have been cut off from the West for too long and they are desperately anxious to catch up with what has been going on there in the last twelve years. Now, at last, they are free to explore the whole field of human knowledge; Western books which used to be locked up have come back to the library shelves. They are free to get on with their personal and intellectual lives. They want to travel and they want to learn all they can. But most of the young people I know are intent on remaining in Poland."

"Would they fight again if needed?"

"Yes, probably, because they are determined not to return to the suffocating grayness of the Soviet-style existence from which they have just liberated themselves. But they would rather get on with their studies."

"What are their prospects after they graduate?" I asked.

"The prospects are rather bleak, unless the economic situation improves," said Estreicher. "Out of the 125,000 who will graduate from universities, high schools and vocational schools all over the country this year, only about twenty-three thousand can expect to find work in the next twelve months. It is a serious situation, as jobless young people are always political dynamite, and Poland is a powder keg that does not need much to explode."

In the next few days, I was to have numerous conversations with the Krakow University students. We talked about books and music and intellectual life in America, of which they knew very little, and of the future way of life in Poland, which they call "Polish socialism." Again I tried to find out what that vague term meant.

"Nobody will be poor," explained Julian, a slender, dark-eyed science student. "Nobody will lack a job; nobody is going to be very rich, but then there will be no poverty. It will be a planned economy, but the people will have a say in what the Party decides. And, above all, there will be freedom—freedom to say and to write what one pleases."

They did not want to copy Western democracy; they did not like what they thought they knew about it. They called it "a ruthless sink-or-swim society," where wealthy idiots often ordered brilliant intellectuals about. They were not interested in the Yugoslav example, but they all wanted to learn more about China.

Most of the young people I met seldom had enough food and nice clothes—and they never had a room of their own. Conditions of their everyday life were miserable. Still, they were incredibly alive, gay and carefree, and adventurous in their minds. It was an exciting prospect to think how much they would learn and unlearn now that Poland was reopening its intellectual frontiers. The Ford Foundation study grant had just been announced, and candidates were already being screened. I looked forward to meeting the boys on American soil and discussing the same subjects again.

There were great gaps in their knowledge of the outside world; but I did not worry about them. The free exchange of thought and ideas will fill those gaps. What I hoped was that they would be left alone and in peace, so they could experiment for themselves in building the humane society of their dreams.

"Now that you are in Krakow," said Estreicher, "you must see Nowa Huta. It is only a few miles from here, and I shall drive you out there tomorrow."

It seemed delightfully incongruous to be guided around Poland's newest industrial development by the curator of Krakow's National Museum.

Nowa Huta (New Mill) is Poland's costliest and most ambitious project, built by the Russians in the middle of the rich Polish farmland with Polish money and labor. Completed in 1954, it is now producing about a million tons of steel products annually—20 percent of the total Polish output. But it is far too big for Polish needs and almost never operates to capacity, as Poland's supplies of steel ore are limited and the deliveries from Russia rarely arrive on schedule.

To house the 25,000 workers, there has sprung up a vast new city where 80,000 people live. This is where, according to Stalinist planners, the new man of Poland was to be bred, formed and forged into a proletariat. He was to be the product of all classes, all parties and all areas of the country. Early in 1949, appeals went out throughout Poland, calling for volunteers to build the "workers' dream city." Fat slogans promised high wages, double food-rations, modern quarters, medical care, entertainment and a dazzling, unclouded future.

So they came from all over Poland: from villages, from cities, from the sandy plains of Mazowsze and the rich agricultural fields of Poznanskie, from fishermen huts on the Baltic and from the mountain slopes of Carpathia. They came in trains, in trucks, on bicycles, on foot and in horse-driven carts. They were young people, men and women, most of them totally unskilled, fleeing the misery of the land and of forced collectivization. While in other parts of the country workers lived on starvation wages and stood in long, dreary lines for rations of bread and potatoes, the builders of Nowa Huta got the best food, new living quarters, cinemas and a large theatre of their own. They were housed in huge, uniform buildings, in individual apartments especially built for them with modern kitchens and baths. Most of them had never seen an electric light before, and the rapid transition from village life to the city was bewildering. So they stared at the brand-new kitchen equipment, the gleaming bathtubs and taps from which flowed running water and wondered, in their bewilderment, whether the tub would prove big enough to store next winter's supply of potatoes, or whether the hen would continue to lay eggs when housed under the kitchen sink. One of the workers refused to part with his goat, and he took her up and down on the elevator each day!

There was in it more than backwardness. The peasant's instinct for self-preservation had been too cruelly abused in the past; they would not any more rely on local shops for supplies. The future proved they were right. When the gigantic industrial project was finally pushed through and the steel plant was up, acute food shortages developed and their supplies of potatoes in the bathtubs came in handy.

We drove around for a while through the muddy, desolate streets. There was not a tree anywhere in this model city of socialism though, according to official statistics, it had 342 stores, 112 workers' coöperatives, shops for tailoring, shoe-making, watch repairing and barbering. Also 14 nurseries, 20 schools, 4 hospitals, cafés, restaurants and bars. No churches.

We stopped in front of one of the gray, dreary blocks—"Block A. Quarter B-32," it said. I decided to have a look at one of the apartments. We went up a narrow stone staircase to the second floor and knocked at the door on the left. A young woman in a rust-colored skirt opened the door. She was pleasant and friendly and, after we had chatted outside for a while, she invited us to come in. The room was small. There was a large iron bed in one corner, a table and a few chairs, pink paper curtains on the window and holy pictures on the walls.

Both she and her husband worked at The Mill, she said, but Thursday was her day off. They had enough money to live on, but not enough for her to stop working. They had been in Nowa Huta for three years, and she was longing to leave it.

"Why do you want to leave Nowa Huta?" I asked. "This is supposed to be the ideal place in the country to work; the wages here are higher than anywhere else."

She gave me an uncertain smile and picked up the shirt she was mending. "It is depressing," she said. "They all drink so much. There isn't much else one can do here. I am always afraid to go out in the street on Saturday night—there are so many brawls."

I thought of the poem by the young Warsaw poet, Wazyk, describing life in Nowa Huta. I had read it in Warsaw a week before. Now it did not seem abstract or remote any more:

> *"From villages, from cities, in trains, on wagons*
> *They come to build a foundry, to build a city . . .*
> *Suddenly awakened from medieval darkness,*
> *A wandering mass, inhuman Poland*
> *Screams with boredom through the December nights.*
> *Here the Vistula flows,*
> *The mob builds industry,*
> *Unknown in Poland, but known to history.*
> *And they are fed on the great empty words*
> *In slow pain, reeling from noxious coal fumes,*

> *Live wildly from day to day, despite the preaching*
> *Being forged into a proletariat.*
> *Meanwhile a mountain of dross. . . ."*

" 'The new man of Poland' proved more difficult to create than the steel mill," said Estreicher, as we got back into the car. "Not until they are given some incentive will these people be able to work better and hope for something else than just to forget reality."

We drove on to the Huta Lenina, the actual steel works. Begun in 1949, this huge industrial complex which is still unfinished was patterned after blueprints purchased from the Soviet Union. The all-automatic equipment was copied after the steel mills of Magnitogorsk and Zaporozhye.

We stood outside for a while, looking at the nine towering stacks. Beyond us lay the ancient village of Czyzyny, its straw-thatched roofs clearly visible in the distance. Across the river to the right stood a tall man-made hill, with a stone eagle carrying a sword in its claws. It was the monument to Wanda, a legendary Polish queen, daughter of Krakus, the founder of Krakow, who had jumped into the Vistula at that very spot, rather than marry the German prince Rüdiger, who was besieging Krakow asking for her hand and her kingdom. The monument had stood there for over a thousand years, surrounded by fertile fields 'and ancient villages, a few miles from Krakow, the capital of the old Polish kingdom.

Now it had Huta Lenina for a neighbor.

I felt sorry for Wanda. After a thousand years, her peace was being disturbed.

On our way back we met entire families walking toward Nowa Huta from church in the adjoining village of Mogila. It was the beginning of Easter Week, and many had walked the four miles to attend evening services.

"I hear there is going to be a church at the Mill this summer," said Estreicher. "There should have been one there before that. Even the Stalinists have known all along that the new man of Poland will refuse to live without God."

We drove back to Krakow along the bumpy highway. As we were entering the city, the trumpeter's "Heynal" was sounded. I was relieved and delighted. Somehow I had been afraid that Nowa Huta might have done something evil to him.

CHAPTER 10

A Socialist Ski Resort

THE road from Krakow twisted and turned running south through a landscape of wooded hills and scanty patches of tilled ground. Pastures covered the hillsides and the crests of the ridges. Spruce forests lined the winding macadam highway on both sides. "Zakopane—35 km." said the crude wooden sign pointing to a bridge suspended over a fast flowing mountain stream. We had just passed Nowy Targ and were heading straight for Zakopane, the picturesque ski resort in the High Tatras, where as a growing girl I had had my first skiing lessons. Often during the past two months I had watched the crowds of eager young men and women walking toward the Warsaw Main Railroad station carrying skis and skiing equipment on their backs. A forest of skis always awaited the arrival of the Warsaw-Zakopane Express. After an overnight journey on the uncomfortable wooden benches, they would awake the next morning in the clear, limpid air of the mountains. For the last 50 years skiing has been Poland's most popular sport. Not even the dreariness of the Stalin era succeeded in abating the country's enthusiasm for it.

"When life gets to be unbearable—there always is Zakopane," Gustaw, Anka's husband, had said just a few days before. "Rail transportation is uncomfortable, but cheap, and the collective lodgings run like the students' hostels are clean, so we all take advantage of the skiing when we can."

The Carpathian Mountains to the south and their continuation, the High Tatras, provide a welcome change of scenery from the wide, open plain, which covers most of Poland. Geographically they form a part of the vast mountain system which extends all the way from Upper Silesia in Germany to the Iron Gate of the Danube, which divides them from the Balkans. The Carpathians, though wild, are not Alpine in character; their slopes are gently rounded, covered with oak, larch and beech-trees with trunks many feet in girth. In autumn, when larches become pale golden and maples turn to red, the mountains take on a splendor of color and light. But the Tatra is different. It is steep and forbidding, like the Alps, with jagged peaks of dark granite and magnificent wide open ski slopes. It has lakes, waterfalls, hidden valleys and a wealth of folklore and old legends. Its people never venture far away from their mountains; they are proud, self-reliant, taciturn and ceremoniously courteous. They cling to their colorful native costumes; and have evolved a distinct architectural style, regional art, music and dance of their own.

Our car was climbing up steadily. Suddenly, as the gates of the forest were thrown open, the sunlit rocky highlands of the Tatra came into view. Soon after we were entering Zakopane. The name means "a place buried in the ground"—probably because the town lies in a small valley surrounded by towering mountains all around.

My last visit to Zakopane was in the winter of 1939. We arrived on the night train from Warsaw with my parents. I still remember the rows of horse-driven carriages at the station, the mountaineer drivers, called the "gazdas," dressed in tight white felt trousers, colorfully embroidered felt capes, round black hats with a feather and the inevitable pipe placed in the corner of the mouth. Their faces were like the sharp outlines of the mountains around them. They were quiet but inevitably polite and could predict tomorrow's weather and snowfall with an accuracy unmatched by any scientific instrument in existence. That winter Zakopane was host to the Internatonal Ski Championship (FIS). Several new hotels had been built for the occasion, a new ski lift and a magnificent ski jump, one of the best in Europe. The town was crowded and throbbing with excitement. Foreign visitors, most of whom had never skied in the Tatras, gaily strolled down the steep, narrow streets, delighting in the magnificent scenery and the endless variety of empty, wide, virgin slopes.

What I remember best of those weeks is a succession of gay, sundrenched days in the snow, the laborious climbs up the mountains, as only one ski lift built to the highest peak— the "Kasprowy"—was available, the carefree shussing down-hill, the music and the warmth of the small mountain inns, where we used to stop on the way down for a cup of hot milk, scrambled eggs or hot punch. I remember the enchanting miracle of crocuses and snowdrops emerging against the chaste background of new grass in the valleys, where the early spring sun had already melted the snow. In the evenings, with large parties of friends, we drove in gay cavalcades of horse-driven mountaineer sleighs up high above Zakopane to remote mountain inns, tucked in forests of spruce. There was candle light and a local band, consisting of a long, narrow violin called *gesliki,* and of a bagpipe, called the *kobza.* We sat on crude, wooden benches sipping mead, or a mild home-distilled cherry brandy, listening to the nostalgic, sometimes harsh local tunes and watched the flickering flames in the huge, roughhewn stone fireplace. Sometimes if the mood was propitious the local men would agree to perform the robbers' dance. Tales of legendary robbers stalk the highlands of Tatra.

As recently as forty-five years ago it was considered unsafe
to travel unescorted along a large stretch of road from
Zakopane to Krakow.

> *"Drink, drink and drive fast past Nowy Targ,*
>   *Once you've passed it you are safe . . ."*

said the popular song.

The legend of Janosik, the fiercely independent leader of
the Tatra robbers is still very much alive. Like Robin Hood,
Janosik is said to have been a symbol of freedom; he refused
to recognize authority. He would have remained undefeated
had it not been for his jealous mistress who betrayed him to
the gendarmes.

The robbers' dance was created in memory of Janosik. It
is a wild dance, performed by men alone, something akin to
the dance of the Cossacks, but wilder. When performed in
the open a leap over a burning fire is one of the necessary
figures. The music is primitive and haunting. It conveys the
distant murmur of the mountain spruces, the howling of the
wind, caught in the granite peaks, the loneliness of the shep-
herds who follow their flocks over the endless expanse of
the pastures.

Some mornings, when the weather was particularly brilliant we visited "Morskie Oko," the "Eye of the Sea," a lake
in the perfect shape of an oval, about 7,000 feet above sea
level. It was beautiful and remote; its dark green, puffy stone
pines, stood silent, like columns of green porfiry against the
granite walls of sheer rock. Awed by the glory of nature
around us we would silently rejoin our sleighs and our quiet,
pipe smoking "gazdas." Back on the sunlit spaces later, we
happily sang mountain ballads.

This time, as we were past the skiing season, there was no
snow left in Zakopane—but the outline of the familiar peaks
brought back my memories. Here was "Giewont," the

mountain in the shape of a sleeping knight in his armor, and "Gerlach," the highest elevation in Poland (8,737 feet), and "Gubalowka," the gentle slope where I took my first skiing lesson. The town seemed to have shrunk and grown shabbier; the picturesque houses with steep roofs were badly in need of paint and new shingles. Zakopane had become "The Capital of the Wczasy" (paid holidays) and practically all the hotels are now owned and run by the State. "Center of Collective Feeding" said the sign over what used to be the fanciest hotel in the place. Its covered terrace with a sweeping view of the mountains was boarded up with planks. "Collective feeding" was obviously taking place indoors these days. In the last few months several private "pensions" had cautiously opened their doors. They were welcomed with joy and enthusiasm.

We put up at the inevitable "Orbis" Hotel and I went for a stroll in the town. Yes, Zakopane had changed. It was no longer carefree, the hand of socialism had left its mark, but it had changed less than most of the other places in Poland. The mountain people were there as before, strolling around in their white felt, gaily embroidered local costumes and there was still music and singing in the little inns tucked away in the shadows of the jagged rocks with white streaks of snow near their summits.

The music of the Tatras differs in spirit and form from melodies of the Polish lowlands. The harmonization is hard and the style of the melodies, though mostly primitive and stern, has a vivid spontaneity and a special tonality of its own.

For centuries the Tatra has exercised a powerful influence on Polish composers. Moniuszko's *Halka,* one of Poland's most popular operas, is the romantic story of a beautiful mountain girl, painted against the background of the Tatra folklore and native music. Poland's beloved great pianist, Ignacy Paderewski, wrote his *Album of the Tatra Melodies.*

Karol Szymanowski, a leader in the revival of Polish regional music, spent most of his life in Zakopane.

It seemed like an exact repetition of the old pre-war pattern when, a few days after my return to Warsaw, I attended a concert at the Warsaw Philharmonic with friends. This was the classic way we used to spend our winters in pre-war Poland—a few weeks skiing in the Tatras and then straight on to Warsaw on the night train to catch the remaining part of what we called the "Warsaw season." One attended the opera and the concert hall and enjoyed the rich variety of Warsaw's theatrical fare. Most of the Warsaw theatres, including the famous "Teatr Narodowy" (National Theatre) which for 200 years had specialized in classic, beautifully staged productions, were destroyed during the Warsaw Uprising. But they had all been put together, brick by brick, while most of the town still lay in ruins.

With a few Polish friends I went to see the "Warsaw 1957" version of Offenbach's operetta, *The Beautiful Hélène*. It was a tremendous success. The audience of the little theatre on Mokotowska Street listened intently, laughed and enthusiastically applauded the sharp political barbs delivered to the tune of Offenbach's engaging music. A witty young writer, Janusz Minkiewicz, used the opera's libretto as a basis for an amusing take-off on the current political problems, personalities and living conditions in Poland. The play opens with a scene at the Royal Palace in Sparta, dominated by Jupiter's temple in the background. A "Greek choir," composed of unruly intellectuals dressed in dark business suits and wearing glasses, refuses to make the usual offerings to Jupiter. "Times have changed," they sing. "We are tired of you, we care nothing about you these days." The disconcerted Greek god, who looks strikingly like Khrushchev, goes away sadly disappointed. The beautiful Hélène, preparing to meet Paris, orders that clothes be sent to her from the "Ciuchy," the rag market in Warsaw, where the contents of U. S. packages are auctioned off. "Hurry up," she says to the slave. "Come back with the latest American rag. I would rather die than be seen by Paris dressed in an outfit from the People's Coöperative in Sparta." In the last act the victorious Paris sails happily away with Hélène. They get off unnoticed because everybody in the Kingdom of Sparta is busy worrying about "how to raise the standard of living" in Poland.

It was an amusing performance; the three long acts went off quickly in spite of the uncomfortable wooden seats and the heat of the crowded, badly ventilated theatre.

"This is a good theatrical season in Warsaw," said my friend Yasia, a charming, elf-like little woman with dark hair and gay, dancing eyes.

"I can't wait to see *The Diary of Anne Frank* with Janina Traczyk in the lead," said her husband.

There are about sixteen theatres in Warsaw, an opera house, two concert halls and several small experimental theatres. The roster of plays this spring included plays by Anouilh and Cocteau, an excellent modern drama by the gifted Polish dramatist Szaniawski, two operettas, one musical, and a performance of the Polish ballet. But *The Diary of Anne Frank* and *Waiting for Godot* were the two current hits of the season. The arrival of the Old Vic Company with Sir Laurence Olivier and Vivian Leigh was eagerly expected in June.

"Warsaw's intellectual climate is as lively as that of Paris," said a newly arrived French diplomat, looking over the broad choice of evening entertainment listed in the Warsaw *Express Wieczorny (Evening Express)*.

For a country that until recently had been cut off from all contacts with the West, the picture indeed was impressive. How anxious the Poles are to maintain these contacts was dramatically illustrated by audiences all over the country during the recent tournée of the Cleveland Symphony Orchestra. Everywhere they were received eagerly and applauded with tumultuously genuine enthusiasm. "A performance like the Cleveland Orchestra concert has never been heard here before," declared the usually caustic and difficult Warsaw musical critics.

"How come?" a woman in the neighboring seat asked me during the Orchestra's concert in Poznan. "I always thought that Cleveland was just another provincial town. How is it that they have an orchestra of such unbelievable excellence?" She went home puzzled and delighted.

One night, during a performance of Szaniawski's *Aszantka*, an unusually good modern drama, I turned around and remarked to a friend that I was amazed to find that every single seat in the theatre had been sold.

"Yes," he said, "our people's love for the theatre, the music and the written word has increased since the war. Together with skiing and soccer, this is their chief entertainment, and today they are more popular than ever."

CHAPTER 11

The End of a Collective

O N A bleak, windy day last spring I stood in front of a barn in the little village of Borkowo in Western Poland and watched the Polish peasants put an end to a Communist fiction. With thoroughness and dispatch, the hated five-year-old local collective was being disbanded. There had been 35 people on it. They had 3 tractors, 12 horses, 18 pigs and a number of cows. They jointly owned a total of over 1,000 acres. Now they were settling accounts and returning to their own pieces of land.

"From now on I shall be on my own," said Bartoszek, a squat, powerfully built farmer, dressed in a brown corduroy jacket and wrinkled black leather boots. "I am happy to work hard as long as it is for myself and the children. Why should I break my back on something that will never be mine? Look at Gniadek," he said, pointing to a bay horse he was leading. "I was forced to give him to the community stable. How I hated to see others work him. I used to listen to his neighing at night and curse because he no longer was mine. Now we are both going home."

He hitched his horse to the cart and drove off along the tree-lined bumpy road.

One memorable night in October the farmers of Poland

heard Wladyslaw Gomulka announce over the radio the end of forced collectivization. Joyously they threw down their tools and went home to celebrate. Next morning they started marking out claims to private property, according to initial investment, work output and length of participation. Spontaneously created village committees ironed out boundary disputes. Soon out of more than ten thousand collectives, less than two thousand remained. Some fell apart overnight; some, like Borkowo, waited for the crops to come in.

I went back to Borkowo a few months after the collective disbanded. It was a warm, sunny day in late spring. The dirt road, full of potholes, leisurely wound its way through a landscape of green pastures and streams mirroring weeping willows. A lapwing flew overhead at great speed and disappeared in the thicket of reeds near the river. A heron strutted solemnly through a buttercup-covered meadow. The light was soft and diffused. I recognized the sandy road lined with poplars which led to the village of Borkowo and the statue of the Virgin Mary standing in a little grassy enclosure at the crossroads. Blue irises and freshly planted begonias surrounded the foot of the statue. It was Sunday afternoon. People sat outside the whitewashed brick and cement houses. Some watched a game of soccer going on in the nearby field. The village looked orderly and relaxed.

I pulled up to the side of the road so as not to attract attention and walked the few hundred yards to the house of Bartoszek. I noticed that a new tar roof had been put on it since my last visit. The squat, round-faced old farmer was sitting on a wooden bench built along the front wall of the house. His arms rested on a crude walking stick solidly implanted in the ground. He was watching a flock of geese, which waddled noisily across the clover field opposite.

"May Jesus Christ be praised," I said. He had not seen me come in. He looked up, shielding his eyes from the sun.

"Ah, that's the lady from New York," he said, taking off his black Sunday cap. "Good afternoon to you and God bless."

I sat next to him on the bench and remarked that things looked nice and prosperous in Borkowo.

"It's all right," he said. "I told you that everything would be different. Every acre of land around here is used up; last year, a fifth of it lay neglected. Even the sandy stretch near the pine-wood has been plowed under for flax. This is all gold for our own pockets!" He tapped the outsize pocket on his britches.

Bartoszek owned about forty acres of land, including a valuable 15-acre stretch of rich "sugar-beet soil."

"Did you acquire more land recently?" I asked.

"Hm-mm," he mused, "well, perhaps." My question was too direct for his taste. "One tries to, but it is difficult; prices have gone up like the devil."

He was right. Land prices all over the country had shot up drastically since October. An acre of good farmland now cost 17,000 slotys (about $650), a near-75 percent increase from the previous year. They were still rising.

What Bartoszek did not say is that he now gets over 300 zlotys ($12) for a meter of wheat in the free market, as against the former compulsory delivery price of 75 zlotys a meter. Some of his wheat still has to be sold to the government at the former low price, but it is a negligible amount compared to the deliveries of last year. Even these small quotas were to be abolished during 1957.

"I did buy two more horses," said Bartoszek, breaking into my thoughts. "My old Gniadek was not enough for the job. God help me, I did it before they quadrupled in price. They came from a farmer near Koscian. Want to see them?"

We walked behind the house to the stable, which housed the horses, the pigs and a cow. At the sound of our voices,

Gniadek and two sturdy companions turned around in their stalls, stared at us, then resumed the absorbing occupation of hay-munching. The older of the newly bought horses was a dark gray mare, beautifully proportioned, with a long, arched neck and a fine bone structure. Much too good for a regular farm horse, I thought. Bartoszek had been watching my face, smiling smugly. "She must have at least 50 percent Arab blood," I remarked.

He beamed. "Ah, I see you know about horses! Somehow I had a feeling that you would. I shall now lead her outside, so you'll be able to see better."

The harmonious animal pranced nervously on the rough cobblestones. It moved with a natural grace, dilating its nostrils as Arabian horses do.

"They told me she had been sired by Flisak," said Bartoszek. Flisak was an Arab stallion, famous before the war. "It's possible, but no certificate can be found. I shall keep her as a brood mare. You know"—and he put his hand confidentially on my shoulder—"she is not what I needed, but somehow the temptation was too strong. Times are getting better, thank God, so I figured I shall perhaps buy a tractor for the farm, but fine horses are very hard to come by."

"I fully agree with you," I told him as we went for a walk in the fields, the horses a spiritual link between us.

I admired the tall, healthy wheat, the acres of well-tended sugar beet, the vegetables stacked neatly, ready for tomorrow's market in town. Bartoszek's two daughters—nice-looking girls in their early twenties—were weeding an acre of turnips near the house. They wore denim shorts and white blouses.

"Emancipation!" Bartoszek pointed out laughingly. "You wouldn't have seen this before the war, would you?"

I agreed that a farm girl in shorts was indeed something new. Farm women used to be the most conservative element in the country: wide skirts, black stockings, kerchiefs were worn for harvesting, hay-raking, weeding, fruit-picking at all times.

"Julka, go and see whether supper is ready," he called to the older of the girls. She was flaxen-haired and well-built. "You are staying with us for the evening meal," he announced. "My wife has been preparing the dinner ever since you arrived. You'll have plenty of time to return to the city before dark."

I said that I would like to stay very much.

"Things are getting better all the time," he went on, as we were circling the field of potatoes. "We can sell anything we want on the free market—and at a very good price. The biggest problem these days is machinery and plenty of fertilizers. A farmer should have his own tractor—we've had enough trouble with POM."

"POM" was the name for the State Machinery Centers which used to supply farmers with tractors. Run by bureaucrats from the city, they were despised by the farmers, who complained that it took several pounds of paperwork to get a tractor to the farm. The ignorance of the Party bosses who ran them was such that they often sent harvesting machines to a farm in the middle of a downpour, expecting the farmer to harvest his wheat unperturbed.

"But do you know what is the best part of this change?" asked Bartoszek, stopping to pull a weed out of a pin-neat row of potatoes. "We get no more visits from the Party. No ignorant city slicker dares to come and tell me what to plant and when to plow my fields for the nation. They would be afraid now." He laughed. "Not that they were not afraid before! I remember when Walenty, my neighbor, chased a Party inspector out of here with a pitchfork because the bastard was telling him how to apply fertilizer to his barley. He knew just as much about it as Walenty knows about knitting. Why, they were even afraid of the mud; and how they abhorred manure! And the paperwork that went on! Each day new orders arrived through the mail. You could have plastered the whole town with the amount of paper we received in a year. Now the Gromada (village council) handles it all very well. And we all speak to each other again," he added, with a mischievous grin.

In the days of the *kolkhoz*, fights and angry disputes were a daily occurrence. Everyone was afraid of being exploited by a neighbor.

At the village pump, a husky young man was filling two wooden buckets with water.

"How is your father, Antoni?" Bartoszek stopped to inquire.

"The heavy cough is subsiding. He should be up and about in a few days," said the youth, swinging a wooden yoke over his strong, wide shoulders. He hooked two buckets of water to each end of the yoke and went off to his house down the road.

"Old Antoni almost killed himself with the excitement of having his own acres again," explained Bartoszek. "He tilled and tilled from dawn until dusk. I told him many times to slow down, but he wouldn't. Well—he almost departed this earth when the spring dampness set in."

I thought of the long hours my father used to spend in his fields engrossed in conversation with one of the villagers, discussing soil composition of a particular plot of land. There was an intimacy between them—a mutual bond of affection for the land that was being tilled. Father did not approve of absentee landowners—numerous among the old landed gentry. He would have agreed with Bartoszek that only those who live on the land and contribute to its development ought to have the right to possess it. The famine of land in prewar Poland was due to unequal distribution and to the wasteful administration of the huge feudal estates—some as large as 400,000 acres—most of which were located in Eastern Poland. In 1921, less than 60 percent of the total farm area belonged to individual farmers. Although steps were taken to redistribute the land between the wars, the individual peasant's passion for his own plot of land remained largely unquenched. The postwar land reforms and wholesale confiscation were a brutal solution taken by the Communist government with the hope of turning all the arable land in Poland into Russian-style collectives.

Curiously enough, most farmers—even the most rabid anti-Communists—approved of the division of the big estates. But they rose with fury and resentment when asked a few years later to surrender their own properties "for the common good of the *kolkhoz.*" The Utopia of Communist agricultural planners dissolved in a wave of universal sabotage. A furious peasantry and a hopeless agricultural mess became the heritage of Stalinist planning. As a result, Poland, which used to be one of Europe's chief granaries, today is unable to feed its own people. One and a half million tons of wheat have to be imported each year.

"Why work? Why invest? What's the use—this land is not mine, anyway," became the prevailing motto on farms.

Bartoszek's wife was standing in front of the house to greet me. She was still dressed in her good black skirt, white blouse and a kerchief she had worn to church for the vespers. The kitchen, with its old-fashioned stove, was dark. I washed my hands in an aluminum washbasin which stood on a chair in the corner. The basin and an outhouse near the stables were the sanitary facilities of the house. The room next door was a combination bedroom-living room and dinette. A wide window with white and yellow paper curtains looked over the stable and the fields. A round table, covered with a machine-lace tablecloth occupied the center of the room. Two iron beds surrounded by holy pictures were squeezed along the wall opposite; a bulky armchair, straight chairs and a wardrobe made it almost impossible to move. There was only one other room in the house.

"Time to build on," said Bartoszek. "If only building materials were available! I have no son, but perhaps Julka's boy will stay on and help me with the farm. She's been going steady for a year," he confided, "a strong lad, just what I need to help me."

Julka was giggling and blushing. The younger sister attentively studied the white nylon blouse of my suit. She had never seen nylon before.

The chicken, fried in fresh butter, was excellent; so was the cucumber salad with sour cream, called "mizeria." We had a fresh strawberry compote for dessert. It was their regular Sunday dinner; like the majority of farmers, they ate well.

I said good-bye to Bartoszek's family with regret and promised to see them again when I returned to these parts. Bartoszek's plans for the future were all made: he was going to buy one more cow—the price of milk on the market had gone up by more than 100 percent; production of milk, butter and eggs was good business. He also would like to buy additional land—up to the 150-acre limit, which was now allowed by the State in that region.

"It makes sense, now that I know I can leave it to the children," he remarked, as I was settling back in my car. "But this time I shall wait for the neighboring PGR (State farm) to disband. Judging by the way it is run, it should have bankrupted long ago. I don't even like to go near it. What a mess! It makes one's hair stand on end."

"Is there much stealing?" I asked.

"Certainly," said Bartoszek. "You must have heard people say, 'Don't steal from a private garden, but rob the collective instead.'"

The PGR was a State-owned and State-run farm adjacent to the village of Borkowy. There were about five thousand of them in the country.

"In a socialist country the State should own a certain percentage of land," declared Mr. Ochab, the Minister of Agriculture, when asked why these inefficient units existed. He admitted that they brought a deficit of over $200 million dollars to the State in 1956.

Some of the State farms were necessary as experimental seed or livestock-breeding stations. Small farmers cannot afford to experiment with new types of fertilizers or grains. But most of them were just ordinary collectives, run with astronomical waste by Party intellectuals from the city. They were being slowly disbanded and sold for private ownership to the farmers.

I drove back as the dark red ball of the sun sank down slowly behind the tall poplar trees. "Wind tomorrow," Bartoszek had said, looking up. He was planning to start on the hay and was glad that the wind would help it to dry.

Next day, on my way back to Warsaw, I watched from the window of my train the tall wheat bleaching richly across the Polish plains. The tough, shrewd Polish peasant, that inveterate capitalist, has managed to produce under private enterprise what may be Poland's biggest harvest since the war.

Fifteen and a half million people—55 percent of Poland's population—live on farms. A year ago, close to 20 percent of the land had lain fallow; now every square of it was being tilled. Only the very weakest collectives—those in deep debt to the State—were hanging on. Communism in Polish agriculture is dead, and everybody, including the Communist bosses themselves, expects that the country will be better for it.

"We too want the farmer to feel that the land he tills is

his own," said Irena Grosz, an attractive, intelligent woman, editor of the peasant newspaper, *Gromada (The Villager)*.

We were having a cup of coffee in her light, airy office in Warsaw, overlooking the Vistula. I had had many talks with Irena. Wife of a famous Communist general, she had been a Communist for a very long time. Passionately interested in farm problems, she had supported the Communist line of the past, but her respect for the soil and for Poland was deep.

"Our biggest problem in the past was the so-called '*To nie moje*' ('This isn't mine') slogan. It meant: 'I couldn't care less.' It was an impenetrable barrier through which the authorities couldn't break. Things have changed radically, now that we've got rid of a crazy system, but at first we had to restrain the farmers from physically wrecking the property of the collectives. Now that they are on their own, they respect what is theirs and care for it lovingly."

Irena looked out on the little boats chugging along on the river. "You can't force human nature; nor can you break the umbilical cord with which our farmer is tied to his soil. We tried to force them and we lost. Now they are happy again and"—she added with a gay laugh—"they are well on the way to becoming Poland's new wealthy class!"

CHAPTER 12

The Polish Jews

WE WERE sitting at the Rarytas Restaurant in Warsaw, enjoying an after-theatre snack of smoked Russian salmon and vodka. Marian, a pleasant-faced newspaperman, with witty, intelligent eyes behind a pair of dark-rimmed spectacles, raised a glass of vodka to me:

"This is our farewell, in case we don't meet again," he said. "My wife and I are leaving soon."

I asked where they were going.

"We are emigrating to Israel," he said. "We hope to get our passports next week."

I was stunned. I had known of course that Marian was Jewish, but he also was Polish—just like any other Pole. He had been born in Poland, as were his parents and grandparents. He thought of himself as a Pole; he spoke a little English, but otherwise no foreign language. Since the end of the war he had had several chances to leave Poland, but he stayed, finished his university studies and was now one of the brightest young editors on a large Warsaw newspaper. His wife was not Jewish; neither of them spoke Hebrew; they were not Orthodox. Why should they want to go and live in Israel?

"It is partly because of the children," said Marian.

"They've been unhappy ever since other children started re-
ferring to them as 'Jewish,' meaning different. Then—there
is the economic situation here. I have a good job at the moment. But suppose that I lose it? It will be hard for me to get
another one—just because I am Jewish. So, after much thinking and deliberation, we finally decided to leave while we
still can. We hope to start a new life over there.

"You see," he went on, fingering the stem of his glass
absent-mindedly, "Poland has always been my country. I
have never known any other, but in the eyes of the Poles we
are a minority—a rather undesirable one at the moment."

His wife sat next to me, looking sad. She was prepared to
follow her husband anywhere, but the thought of leaving
friends, moving to a totally foreign country and having to
learn Hebrew was scarcely appealing to her. In Israel it was
she who would be in the minority. I felt sorry for them. The
whole situation seemed unreasonable and unjust.

Was Marian exaggerating? Did he carry an oversensitive
chip on his shoulder? The questions are hard ones to answer.

Anti-Semitism very definitely exists in today's Poland. The
government condemns it, the press criticizes it violently, the
people are ashamed of it. But the feeling is fairly widespread,
though its virulence has been exaggerated abroad.

How is it possible that the Poles are still anti-Semitic, now
that they are left with barely twenty thousand Jews out of
a pre-war population of over three and a half million, and
after they've witnessed Nazi atrocities against the Jews perpetrated under their very eyes? Soon after they occupied
Poland, the Nazis built walls around the Jewish quarter of
Warsaw, herding over two and a half million Jews into it.
Three years later they ruthlessly burned the compound to
the ground.

The effect on the Poles was revulsion. Thousands of people
rushed to the assistance of the persecuted race. They fed

them, took them into their homes and hid them, although the penalty for sheltering a Jew in those days was death. On the ruins of the Warsaw ghetto in Muranowska Street stands a powerful monument, cast in bronze, with sculptures in bas-relief describing the living hell suffered by Polish Jews. The Polish people have helped to erect the memorial. So why the dislike again, instead of solidarity and compassion?

The answer is a discouraging one for a nation that prides itself on its tolerance and high ethical standards.

There has always been anti-Semitism in Poland and there will probably always be some, though the feeling today is far less strong than it was a generation ago, when the reasons for it were mostly economic.

Of course not all of the population shares these feelings; thousands of Poles indignantly condemn them; even before the war there always was admiration for the Jews' contribution to the artistic and intellectual life of the country. Some of Poland's best loved poets were Jews; its most famous and most admired actors and pianists were Jewish. "Warsaw would be a very sad place without the Jews," the theatre-lovers of Warsaw used to observe wistfully; this is exactly what many of them are saying again today.

But the sad truth is there, staring everybody in the face: the traditional, shamefully profound anti-Semitism of the Poles remains deeply entrenched in spite of the drastic historical upheavals of the last twenty years.

Had the Germans won World War II, the Polish Jews would have been completely liquidated. It was therefore understandable that after the defeat of the Nazis they turned to the Communists for protection. The Russian-imposed Communist regime in Poland, on the other hand, faced with a generally hostile attitude of the nation, was short of administrative cadres; it welcomed the services of the Jews.

As a result, Jews filled vast numbers of important govern-

ment and administrative jobs. They controlled the Secret
Police (the head of it was Jakub Berman, a Jew), economic
planning, numerous ministries and hundreds of administrative
posts in the provinces. Not all of them were qualified for
their jobs.

When the "moment of truth" came in October, a wave of
hitherto suppressed anti-Semitism suddenly bubbled up to the
surface. It came in spite of the fact that many Jewish intellectuals had been in the forefront of the fight for liberalization.

Together with the freedom of speech came the startling
discovery of the depth of the economic catastrophe. Hilary
Minc, Poland's longtime economic czar, was just one of the
many Jews blamed for ignorant policies which brought the
country to the verge of economic ruin.

In the meantime anti-Semitism in Russia has been steadily
increasing. The Russian Communist Party openly admits its
hostility to the Jews. The same feelings are shared by the pro-
Russian, so-called "Stalinist" faction within the Polish Communist Party in Poland. Having suffered a resounding defeat
in October, the "Stalinists" were casting about for a popular
slogan, which would turn the country's attention away from
the dismal reality for which many of them were being
blamed.

"The Russians are innocent. The Jews are responsible for
the mistakes of the last twelve years," they proclaimed. It
was a clever maneuver and initially very successful.

But the Government of Gomulka stepped in and blocked
it in time. In one of his very first pronouncements Gomulka
appealed for an end to the anti-Semitic slogans and warned
that demonstrators would be severely punished. Today the
government admits frankly that, in spite of all its efforts, the
anti-Jewish feeling persists. With the help of the press, it
tries to counteract and control it.

In the meantime many people have suffered. Jews who returned to Poland after the end of the war, because it was *their* country, hoped to remain there forever. Now they are confused; they have doubts as to their usefulness and plan to emigrate while they can. Many have changed their names to make them sound Polish.

In Krakow I talked to a Jewish girl who had just returned from abroad. She could have stayed there, she told me, but she *preferred* to return to Poland. She had been in Krakow barely a month when a relative asked that she change her name to one that would make people think she was Polish. She refused. Her parents died in a German concentration camp because they were Jewish, she said, and she was going to retain their name. But as time went on, she noticed that some of her friends, when introducing her to strangers, had been pronouncing her name in an unintelligible way so as to disguise the fact it was Jewish. Gradually she became aware of the mounting anti-Semitism around her. With a heavy heart she decided to leave Poland and emigrate to Israel.

There are many like her. The Jewish community in Poland, which for seven hundred years had been a vital part of Polish economic and cultural life, is rapidly disappearing.

The exodus is spurred on by two factors: one is the extreme sensitivity of the average Polish Jew and his frequent persecution complex; the other is the powerful attraction of the prosperous, well-organized State of Israel. Life in Poland is hard for Poles and non-Poles alike. The struggling Jewish merchant or small government official who lost his job, not because he was Jewish but because of the current cutback in governmental institutions, sees in the growing prosperity of Israel a magic spot on earth where he will settle down and live happily.

The aura of heroism which surrounds a victim of political persecution will not be a detriment, he may reason. During a recent reduction in the staff of a large Polish newspaper, over twenty people lost their jobs. The three Jews among them applied immediately for passports to emigrate on the grounds of "political persecution."

Not all the Jews feel that way; there are still about twenty thousand left in Poland who, in spite of everything, have decided to remain in *their* country.

"I have no intention of emigrating," a leading Jewish newspaperwoman, mother of two children, said to me. "This is a passing phase, and things are not really as bad here as we Jews represent them to be. Anti-Semitism comes from Russia. The Polish press tries hard to combat it. The center of anti-Jewish propaganda in Poland is the Soviet Embassy in Warsaw."

She was right. When the present wave of resentment, fanned in deviously intricate ways by the Russians, subsides, the shrunken Jewish community in Poland will probably become integrated into the national life of the country, prepared to see things through no matter what the uncertain future may bring.

I saw Marian and his wife again at the Cleveland Orchestra concert in June. The floor of the Warsaw Philharmonic was throbbing with public enthusiasm, as thousands of pairs of clapping hands greeted the brilliant playing.

Marian and Renata were enthralled. "What a wonderful farewell this has been," said Renata.

"Are you really going to leave in a week?" I asked her.

"Yes, we are," said her husband. "Wish us luck!"

CHAPTER 13

The Poznan Fair

J UNE was a busy month because of the International Fair at Poznan, which opened its gates during the first weekend. The KLM, the Sabena and the Scandinavian airlines which operate biweekly flights into Warsaw altered their schedules to stop in Poznan for the convenience of foreign businessmen who were converging on the city by the hundreds. It was Poznan's 26th International Fair—a traditional event held each year in June, with the exception of the war years. Memories were still fresh of the previous June, when Poznan workers, taking advantage of the presence of foreign businessmen in their town, revolted against the Soviet brand of Communism which for twelve years had brought them nothing but hunger and poverty. Four months later, the new era of freedom—if not of prosperity—was ushered in.

In 1957, for the first time, the U. S. Government participated in the Fair. Everyone in the country—from members of the Government down to the average Pole—was anxious to see what the United States would show them.

The day before the opening of the Fair, I drove the 150 miles from Warsaw to Poznan with John and Margareth Berg of our Embassy in Warsaw. In the car with us was an important consignment—two burlap bags full of American nickels for the automatic vending machines at the U. S. Pavilion at the Fair. We drove across a flat, wooded country, passing well-tended fields, high healthy wheat, neat rows of potatoes and greens. Fruit-heavy cherry trees bordered long stretches of road. As usual, there was no traffic, though this was the *autostrada*, Poland's most modern highway, connecting Berlin with Warsaw.

We stopped for a picnic lunch at the edge of a wood. The day was warm and the air was fragrant with clover.

Margareth stretched her pretty young figure on the grass and contentedly lit a cigarette. "I used to be very unhappy when we first came to Poland a year ago," she said. "Everything seemed bleak and hopelessly poor. I longed for John to be transferred to another post. But I have come to like it—this country grows on you, though I can't quite explain what it is. I suppose it's the people; their spontaneity, zest for life and their interest in everything Western. Now that they feel free to talk and come to our house, I look forward to having Polish friends at last."

The Bergs, like other U. S. Embassy personnel, live in a spacious, comfortable house bought and furnished by the U. S. Government for American dependents overseas. They have three small children, all of whom speak fluent Polish.

Before October, families of American diplomats in Warsaw led a restricted existence. Their social and cultural activities were limited to other Americans, diplomats or foreign correspondents. No Pole would dare invite them to his house; even visiting the American Embassy on business was risky. Polish servants employed by American families were regularly called to the secret police for "reporting." The atmosphere was one of suspicion and gloom. Now the oppressive curtain has been lifted. Warsaw has become much like any other Western European post—in atmosphere, though not in comfort. Even Colonel Marley, the jovial, round-faced Air Attaché, reported that his car was no longer being followed during his regular trips into the countryside.

On a long stretch of straight road near Kutno, we passed two Russian lorries going in the direction of Warsaw. Russian soldiers sat silent and gloomy on uncomfortable wooden benches. They were part of a local detachment servicing the telephone lines between Warsaw and Legnica in Southern Poland, where sixty thousand Russian troops are stationed.

"They are billeted in peasant houses in villages along here and told to be as inconspicuous as possible," said John Berg. "I must say, one is not very conscious of their presence in Poland."

I reflected again on how tenuous is Poland's hard-won independence. To the casual observer, the country appears sovereign and free. But one glance at the map immediately reminds one of the one hundred or more Russian divisions looming menacingly at the border, about ninety miles east of Warsaw; of the thirty divisions stationed in East Germany, on Poland's western flank; and of the large Russian contingent in Legnica, in Southern Poland. This lonely self-sustaining unit is packed into a perimeter of about thirty-five miles; the soldiers are forbidden to move freely around the countryside. Because of that, Poles often forget about the existence of the Russian armies on their soil. But they are there—a grim reminder that it is not easy for a nation in Poland's geographical position to slip completely away from the embrace of the Colossus.

Poznan appeared in the distance—a mass of gray stone buildings in a heavy-set German style. I remembered it well. We lived less than one hundred miles from it and used to drive to Poznan frequently to see doctors, buy clothes or visit friends in the surrounding countryside. We also liked the Poznan Zoo, which had more elephants than any other zoo in Europe. For over a hundred years Poznan had been a German city; it retained much of the stolid, orderly characteristics of the Germans. Though largely industrial, it has a fine old university and several comfortable hotels. We passed the stone bridge over the River Warta and turned left into the old market square, heading for the Bazar Hotel in the center of the town. The wide well-swept streets were decorated with flags of the thirty-one nations participating in the Fair.

The Bazar Hotel—repainted, replastered and redecorated for the occasion—was a scene of confusion. Every foreign diplomat or businessman in Poznan was anxious to stay there, but the hotel had only eighty rooms—and five baths. Its hallway, decorated in black-and-white Polish marble, was stacked solid with American, British, French and German-made luggage. I went across the square to the Poznanski Hotel, where some of the foreign correspondents were billeted, and after a considerable wait was assigned to a tiny dark room with a small narrow bed and no bath. I was glad to have it. Though the Poznan Municipal Council had guaranteed to house every foreign guest to the Fair, there were only slightly over eight hundred beds available in the town—and more than a thousand guests had already arrived.

The streets outside the hotel were crowded. There were consumer goods in the windows, more varied and attractive than in Warsaw. Fresh paint, fresh flowers and gay multicolored flags gave the town a carnival-like atmosphere. People were milling around admiring the foreign cars parked in front of the Bazar and the Poznanski. But underneath it all there was tension. Poznan was wary and watchful. June of a year ago was on each person's mind.

Fred Tappin, an English businessman, was puffing on a cigarette in the lobby. "It was hot like today," he recalled.

"I was staying at the Poznanski, on the same floor as this time. I awakened suddenly around eight o'clock in the morning to the noise and confusion of a crowd on the march. I ran to the window and could hardly believe my eyes. There were thousands of men—it seemed as if the whole city in its ragged attire was marching under the hot sun—chanting: 'WE WANT BREAD.' I must say, it was enough to cast a glance at their shoes to understand the profound reason for the demonstration!

"I had to drive to the market place that morning. When I returned two hours later, buses and trolleys had stopped in their tracks, and conductors and passengers had joined in the demonstrations. My English car, flying a Union Jack, was applauded, and they let me through to the hotel without difficulties. When I got there, the initial demonstration of the sixteen thousand Cegielski workers had become that of the whole city. Homes and schools and offices emptied and joined the demonstrators. It was so sudden that it seemed to have been perfectly organized. Even the police let things alone—at first. But as the crowds increased, their slogans grew more demanding. Standing here in front of the Bazar, I heard such incendiary remarks as 'Out with the Russians!' and I saw Soviet flags torn down and trod underfoot. Soon we saw armored cars and heard machine-gun fire. Tragedy broke out at twenty minutes past ten. The intensity of the fire drove us back into the hotel. We knew what the eventual outcome would be and we were heartsick."

The Poznan uprising was finally smothered with tanks. But before that, for three days this stolid city of 370,000 inhabitants fought furiously, knowing that it could not attain victory nor hope for it.

The fallen of Poznan chose to die under the eyes of the West, that their death might bear witness. It was good to note, now, a year later, that foreign visitors were here once again and that there was no longer need for the people to whisper when talking to them in public places. Poznan of 1957 was far from happy and satisfied: the economic situation was still desperate, but at least there was freedom to grumble.

Still . . . the graves of the fallen were fresh, and the anniversary of the battle was nearing. Hence, the tenseness.

"The opening of the Fair is tomorrow at 10 A.M. I will give you a lift in my car if you are up on time," said New York *Times'* Sydney Gruson. He locked the doors of his sky-blue Plymouth station wagon, which was attracting crowds of mechanically minded Polish admirers.

We drove to the Fair the next morning.

Poznan is rightly proud of its fair grounds. Built in the early 1920's, when Poland was still recovering from the ravages of World War I, they were a gigantic achievement for an economically weakened nation. "They are well planned, as big as Wembley but much prettier," said a visiting English businessman, an old-time exhibitor at the Fair.

This year thirty-one countries packed their products into the forty-acre grounds. For the first time Western nations dominated the show. They took up three-quarters of the space; last year they took only half.

A huge steel tower, initialed U.S.A., was visible in the distance from the Fair's entrance gate. We slowly made our way toward it, passing, without a backward glance, places that offered one iced beer, frankfurters, shaded chairs, Swiss cheeses, Greek wines, West German machinery, Czechoslovakian glassware and enchanting Polish wood carvings.

Under a huge 124-foot-diameter dome rising like a fat half watermelon fifty feet above the fair grounds, a tall, heavyset, completely bald man stood watching a display of

American ready-made clothes (mostly from Ohrbach's) modeled by pretty Polish girls. "A fine example of Polish-U. S. coöperation," mused Polish Premier Jozef Cyrankie-wicz. He was spending the greater part of his visiting time at the U. S. Pavilion. He moved on to an outdoor turntable on which stood a gleaming selection of U. S. 1957 "power model" cars with prices posted on them.

"We shall never tear him away from that Lincoln Continental. Look at the glint in his eyes," whispered a Polish journalist accompanying the Premier.

The American exhibit, which was to become a smash hit at the Fair, consisted of an aluminum framework over which had been hung a silvery nylon tent, and of a model house and carport, called a "typical average American's home." Displayed under the dome and in the model six-room, one-story house were the products of over 350 different U. S. manufacturers.

It was a dazzling sight.

A plastic eighteen-foot swimming pool, with an aluminum boat equipped with an outboard motor floating nonchalantly on it, greeted the sun-weary crowds. Around the edges of the pool, on a green carpet of grass, lay water skis, skin-diving equipment, floats, colorful plastic balls, tents, sleeping bags, camp chairs and a portable outdoor grill. Next to it was a display of fishing gear—rods and reels for salt and fresh water, photographs of American sportsmen reeling in gigantic sailfish from Atlantic waters. "Thirty-four million Americans hold hunting and fishing licenses," said a poster close to the Hall of Recreation's entrance. "Fifty million Americans visit the country's national parks each year, enjoying public facilities for camping and hiking," said another Department of Commerce poster.

There was an impressive display of baseball and football

equipment, and photographs of intercollegiate games. Tennis, soccer, ice hockey, archery, bowling, boxing, ping pong, roller skating, golf and skiing gear stared at the goggling crowds.

For "indoor leisure" there were phonographs and radios of all sizes; RCA, Admiral and Westinghouse television sets, and all the latest in U. S. electronics research. There were magazines and newspapers and mail-order catalogues and paperbound volumes of books on all subjects.

The Birds Eye Division of the General Foods Corporation sent a home economist to Poznan to demonstrate the preparation and serving of 264 frozen foods donated by the entire U. S. food industry. Assisted by fourteen English-speaking Poznan University students, Miss Barbara Sampson served orange juice, roast beef, barbecued chicken, glazed ham with frozen peas, and ready-mix cakes to an audience of skeptical Polish housewives. Some of the Polish girl demonstrators were at first afraid to handle the frozen food packages with bare hands and insisted on using pot-holders.

A spiraling staircase led to a balcony under the big nylon dome. Ohrbach's of New York City, the Singer Sewing Machine Company and Bates Fabrics (wrinkle-resistant) held forth here. Pretty Polish girls were hard at work demonstrating how to use the complicated attachments on the sewing machines; models wearing Ohrbach's dresses, "$20 and under," pranced among displays of Bates textiles. There were women's hats, gloves, lingerie and a wide assortment of shoes with prices posted on them.

A flagstone path led to the model house: a three-bedroom, one-floor wooden structure with sliding doors made of California redwood. It was a lovely house, airy, comfortable and cheerful. The large L-shaped living room with a dark brown sofa and blue easy chairs had a picture window looking over a garden full of plants. There was a Hi-Fi record player in one corner and a TV set next to it. A parquet floor with area rugs made the room smart and opulent-looking. The master bedroom was done in tones of yellow, white and beige; the adjoining bathroom was pink-tiled. The child's room next to it—red, and black with royal blue accents, a Navajo rug on the floor and toys stacked on shelves all around it—looked as if Santa Claus had descended the night before. The baby's room, with its bassinette, diaper-disposal unit, intercom system to record whimperings, was a picture out of a model-nursery ad. The kitchen was beige and dazzling—an electric stove, refrigerator, disposal unit, dishwasher, clothes washer and drier were lined up in an imposing array. There were aluminum pots, silver, china and glassware—pot-holders, wax paper, metal foil, dish towels, "miracle cleansers"—all the accoutrements of a well-stocked American household.

Out in the back of the house was a home workshop stuffed with power tools. A Polish employee of the American Pavilion, dressed in gray slacks and a white dacron shirt, ran a nonstop demonstration of a "typical American power mower."

This was not exactly "an average workingman's dwelling." It belonged to the $20,000-a-year higher-income group. The house alone—the Fair authorities said—was worth about $17,-000 without the land. The gadgets and furnishings in it would come to about half as much. But, on the other hand, it *could* be owned by a skilled worker. He could pay for the house in ten years while living in it.

"It is our intent to show Polish Fair goers the enormous range of commodities, foods, clothing and appliances which are within the average U. S. citizen's reach and which in their totality reflect the American standard of living," said a representative of the U. S. Department of Commerce, which spent over half a million dollars on the U. S. exhibit.

Polish crowds pressing into the U. S. Pavilion were not

only impressed—they were awed. It was the bewilderment and disbelieving wonder of a Cinderella appearing at the ball, or Alice in Wonderland looking through the Queen's opera glass. They came, looked, took it all in, went away—their heads buzzing—and returned several times to look again, to see if "it was all real." There was not the remotest connection between the life of a Polish factory worker, his bare one-room apartment, his salary barely sufficient to feed a wife and a child and this wonderland of gadgets, Hi-Fi sets, television, toys, fresh-cut flowers, comfortable furniture—all spread over a living area which in Poland is shared by at least five families. Yes, they knew these things were available in the United States—they had many relatives who told them—but they just refused to believe that "this was the way most American workers lived."

This in my opinion is where the Department of Commerce went wrong. The objective was to tell the story of our free economy and modern America to a people shackled by a planned socialist system. Such was successfully achieved. But by insisting that the big, luxuriously fitted house, the array of power tools in the carport and the gigantic deep freeze were "average sights in a workingman's home," we invited straight disbelief and undermined the public's confidence in our essential thesis—that in a capitalist economy all these things are within a workingman's reach, particularly if his credit is good.

There is no question, however, that the American exhibit was the sensation of the Fair. The attendance figures proved it. Quoting from an official report: "The attendance at the American exhibit was ten times higher than that of any other of the thirty-one exhibiting nations." It reached 100,000 the first day, 85,000 the second, 125,000 the sixth day and ran on a steady average of 90,000 daily. As compared with this, the attendance at the Soviet Pavilion on the opening day of the show was under 42,000, in spite of the many official visitors and free passes.

Part of the American attraction was the fact that, unlike West Germany or the British, we showed little heavy machinery, no locomotives, no harvesters. We did not treat the Fair as an opportunity to do business, as did all other countries. Instead, we showed pretty dresses, frozen fruit juice whipped into drinkable condition by a mixmaster; frozen waffles popping in and out of giant toasters, and a forest of vending machines which dropped out candy bars, hot soup, hot chocolate, soft drinks, cigarettes—all this to the accompaniment of loudly blaring jukeboxes where one could buy a tune for a nickel. The four thousand nickels we brought from Warsaw with us were in constant demand. They were supposed to last for the duration of the Fair, but half of them disappeared after a week. Polish men and women retained them as souvenirs of a "visit to America."

I watched a Polish family—husband, wife and two children—walk through the model house. The pressure of humanity around them was such that they had to move along fairly fast. They were both in their thirties. His face was tanned and alert; she was small, with brown hair, and dressed in a neat blue-and-white print dress.

"I was here yesterday," said the woman. "Do you know what that man standing there told me?" She pointed to a Polish employee working at the U. S. Pavilion. "He said that in America people could have a house like this one by paying for it in monthly installments, like rent. After fifteen or twenty years they own it."

"What if the man loses his job or gets sick?" asked the husband.

"I don't know, but I bet they must have thought of that, too," she said.

We laboriously made our way through the kitchen.

"They say American clothes need no ironing," said the woman. "You know, like the slips and the shirt Hania sent me from New Jersey. These machines look tricky to operate, but imagine never having to wash sheets by hand or dry them! It's good to see things like this once in our lives. Why is the *Gazeta Poznanska* so angry about this exhibit?"

"Oh, it's the same old story," said the husband. "*They* (the ubiquitous *they* of Communist-ruled lands) cannot make things like this, so they try to push off their resentment on the people. Wladek tells me that he has always known Americans had these things. He was liberated from a German camp by the American Army."

I lost them at the exhibit of toys. Pulled ahead by their impatient youngsters, they were last seen gazing admiringly at a miniature electric speedboat. The crowd in the toyland was dense. Few toys are manufactured in Poland. They do nothing for the economy, say the planners. Starry-eyed Polish youngsters took up positions in the U. S. toyland and refused to be budged by their parents.

A tall man in worker's pants and an open-neck shirt pulled out a handful of dollars from his pocket. "Let me have that dancing bear," he said gruffly. His disappointment was immense when told the toys were not for sale.

Many people came up to various exhibit stands carrying wads of dollars in their hands—part of the great reservoir of greenbacks that is almost a second currency in Eastern Europe. Some of the bills were more than fifty years old.

"Let's have lunch in America," I overheard a couple say, making their way to a square of unoccupied lawn at the back of the American "dream house." They obviously had come straight from the vending-machine paradise. He carried two paper cups full of freshly whipped orange juice; she had a bag of sandwiches in one hand and a paper cup of hot chocolate in the other. They settled down happily between alternate sips of orange juice and hot chocolate.

Two soldiers and an elderly woman were talking to a Polish-speaking attendant. "How much does a washing machine cost in the United States?" asked the woman.

He told her.

"What is it in terms of a workingman's pay?" asked the soldier.

"About two weeks," was the answer.

"Just as long as it takes here to buy a not-so-good pair of shoes. You know," said the young soldier pushing back a lock of blond hair from a perspiring forehead, "you people should have put these facts right over the exhibits. There is a Polish-made washing machine. It takes just one sheet and two pillow cases; it costs 4000 zlotys—four months' pay."

It is impossible, of course, to buy anything like American kitchen equipment in Poland. New kitchens in the new workers' apartments have a coal range and cold water only. The government allows a ton and a half of coal to heat one room in the winter. It costs about eight days' labor. But in order to get through the winter, the worker must buy another ton and a half—on the black market. There is no refrigeration of any kind in the homes; few electrical appliances exist.

No wonder Communist newspapers attacked the American exhibit as "boastful"! They called it a "rich man's show to impress a hard-working but poor man." But the passing throngs obviously enjoyed being impressed. They liked the feel of the American fabrics, the gleam of the new refrigerators and the electric ranges, the taste of the cooked frozen peas—even the blare of the American jukeboxes. They were items out of the ordinary Pole's reach—not in a thousand years could he hope to live in a house comparable to the one he was seeing, he thought; but, on the other hand, he did not

quite believe that "such a house" was "easy to acquire." The
very opulence of our show failed to make it applicable.

There was some criticism mixed in with admiration. The
frozen "TV dinners" which an American family can eat while
watching its favorite show greatly impressed Mr. Cyrankiewicz, the Prime Minister, but drew acid remarks from a number of mothers who thought it a disastrous habit, ruinous to
a child's appetite and good manners. The stainless-steel table
utensils on the dream kitchen's table were puzzling to many.
"Why, with all this luxury, they surely could afford to have
silver! Only the very poor eat off steel."

Some women were disappointed that not enough "high-
style fashions" were shown; some criticized children's clothes
as "made for little grownups," not for children.

The Polish Fair management was disappointed at the lack
of heavy industrial machinery.

But these were just isolated ripples. The overwhelming impression of Mr. and Mrs. Poland, trooping lightheartedly
through the 50,000 square feet of transplanted America, was
one of curiosity and amazement.

By comparison with the triumphant United States, the
Soviet exhibit ran far behind. Its location was poor—at the far
end of the grounds. Apparently the Russians had made up
their minds to participate in the Fair very late, and this year
they did not dare to demand the choicest location. As in the
U. S. Pavilion, their emphasis was on consumer goods. But
how could the square-shouldered, heavy-set Russian models
compete with the well-cut, snappy American-styled dresses?
The fashion-conscious Polish women did not even stop to
look closer. "I would not be caught dead in one of *those*
horrors," was the average viewer's opinion.

Several Polish people amused themselves at playing a sort
of "Let us annoy the Russians" game. Before entering the

Russian Pavilion they would agree on what to say that would be most annoying to the Soviet Union. Some jeered, some made loud deprecating remarks in Russian.

They were enjoying their freedom with a vengeance.

At the West German Pavilion I ran into my friend Roman, talking to Polish Government officials. "Have you seen the Russian Pavilion?" he asked. "They do not have any caviar this year, but they have a new camera modeled after the German Leica. It is mechanically perfect and very inexpensive, I hear. Let's see."

We walked to the Russian exhibit coming in face to face with rows of Khrushchev's corn in large tins. A cream-colored car named the Volga, with white tires and a curiously high-perched undercarriage, occupied the center of the room. Around it spread fine Oriental rugs. Beyond was an unending display of heavy machinery.

We found the camera, which looked like an exact if rough copy of a Leica and cost about $35, complete with a light meter. Under a huge sign saying *Radio*, three Russian TV sets lined together reflected three different views of Prime Minister Cyrankiewicz visiting the Soviet exhibit. It was a clever gimmick, attracting crowds of spectators. Cyrankiewicz's heavy pale face and bald head (he had lost all his hair in a German concentration camp) showed boredom and perspiring weariness from the heat.

We agreed that from a propaganda point of view the 1957 Soviet exhibit was a complete washout. Opening-day rumors had it that the Russians had complained to photographers that too few of them were around.

We joined a group of Polish newspapermen and tramped around the fair grounds for hours. We visited the British Pavilion, with its woolens, textile machinery, gaily colored buses and small cars; we sampled wines and admired the filmy lingerie and the sweaters at the French and the Austrian pavilions; the dazzling array of Greek fruit was a welcome relief after the East German sausages and cooked meats. We saw the impressive array of locomotives of the Henryk Cegielski works at Poznan. Last year a State export agency displayed the same Cegielski products, and the name of the factory was Stalin Works. This year they had an independent stand at the Fair. We bought Polish wood carvings, drank West German beer and listened to organ music at the East German Pavilion.

The atmosphere of the Fair was carefree. It was a lovely June day; people looked gay, summery and relaxed. Thoughts of revolution and violence seemed far away and unreal. But as we drove back to the hotel, the number of police everywhere reminded us that the anniversary of the riots was nearing and that the authorities were taking no chances.

Two weeks later, just a few days before the anniversary of the 1956 uprising, the Poznan Fair closed its gates. The United States emerged with a propaganda victory. Sales triumphs went to the West Germans and the British. More than 900,000 people had passed through the U. S. Pavilion, many two or three times in one day. Some said they had come miles to the Fair to demonstrate their friendship for the West and especially for America. The upper floor of the American exhibit had to be closed for a day and reinforced because it was feared the weight of the crowds would cause it to collapse.

We did not do much actual business. Unlike all other countries at the Fair, we did not try very hard. But as one of our Commerce Department officials remarked, "Next year we are really going to talk trade." Polish exporters who heard him hoped this was going to be so.

Probably the most significant U. S.-Polish transaction at the Fair was the purchase of $4000 worth of Polish crystals by two Polish-American ladies from Milwaukee, who quietly came to the Fair "just to see," liked the crystals and took them home to Milwaukee because "so many of us like to have things from Poland in our homes."

The British concerns, aided by bank credits to Poland of close to $140,000,000, gained big orders for textile machinery, tractors and harvesters. A British tractor company completed a deal so large that it decided to open its own service stations in Poland.

On the whole, the Fair was a blessing for Poland because of the resulting trade agreements. Contracts calling for exports of over 54.7 million dollars' worth of Polish goods—mainly coal, locomotives and machine tools—were signed by the Polish Government. Its best customer was a Western nation—Great Britain.

"This is a tremendous step forward from last year, when we could only hope to sell our wares to Soviet Russia or China—or perhaps East Germany. We are moving along the right road—if only we're allowed to continue undisturbed," a Polish journalist said to me.

It was a very big "if." It looked as if Poland's economic position was to continue desperate for a long time to come. With it went the ever-present possibility of an explosion.

In spite of the dynamite in the air, there was visible improvement. We talked about it one night of the Fair at the Syrena (Siren) cabaret in Poznan.

We were a mixed group: a Polish Communist writer for the government publication, *Trybuna Luda,* and his fiancée; Colin Frost of the Associated Press, an experienced newspaperman with the mobile face of a young unruly boy. He was suffering from a violent headache at that moment and was taking what he called "vodka pills" to relieve it. There was Lisa Larsen, photographer for *Life,* who perplexed Polish Government officials because they never got used to the fact that a good photographer could be an attractive young

woman as well. Also, there were an American businessman
from the mid-western states, a long-time customer at the
Fair, Sydney Gruson, Ronald Preston of the London *Times*
as well as others who came drifting by.

Around us American jazz reigned supreme. Polish girls
dressed in pretty summer cottons, their hair well groomed
and shiny, danced away, smiling at their well-scrubbed part-
ners wearing open-neck shirts. They seemed not to have a
care in the world. Last year they were marching in grim
protest. But this June all was serene and forgotten. They were
anxious to forget very quickly—as long as the little they had
now would go on.

I danced with the Communist writer; he danced well. His
pale triangular face, ordinarily watchful and observing, was
relaxed. He looked at the pretty girl, his fiancée, dancing with
Sydney Gruson next to us, and a nice friendly smile spread
from under the thick, round glasses on his face. He was not
going to talk the Communist lingo at us; this June we were
closer to him than his fellow Communists from abroad. At
last we could all enjoy the same things.

The waiter who brought us the drinks greeted Sydney
and Colin with delight. "I remember you, Messrs. Correspondents," he beamed. "You were here last year in September, when the trials of the insurgents were on. I used to serve
you breakfast at the Bazar Hotel every morning. There were
only a few of you at that time, but now the town is full of
visitors from the West. May God make them come here more
and more!"

He went off bowing, one big smile.

The jazz had changed into rock and roll. The American
businessman at our table was squeezing a Polish mannikin
from the Fair. His wife had been calling him from the States,
afraid for Papa's safety in the foreboding Communist land.

He was fine; to him this year Poznan again was a pretty good place to be in.

We walked back to the hotel across the flower-banked Freedom Square. The night was warm. Leisurely walking crowds filled the streets, though the hour was well past midnight. Streetcars clanged by noisily. There was laughter and animated talk in the air.

CHAPTER 14

The Trial of Kazik Mirski

HE STOOD about five feet eight—a frail, middle-aged man with thinning blond hair and a quietly detached expression on his face. In a low, steady voice he answered questions put to him by the judge, then sat back in the witness box, folding his hands across his chest, and resumed gazing pensively into space. The huge whitewashed courtroom was empty of spectators except for a group of relatives and friends who clustered in the first two rows near the window. They had come to watch Kazik Mirski's rehabilitation trial.

Five years ago the Communist Government of Poland had declared Kazik Mirski a traitor because of his wartime service in the underground army and his participation in the Warsaw uprising. Released from captivity by the Germans, he was arrested by the Communists and sent to jail for eight years. Everything he and his family had owned was confiscated by the State. Last autumn, after the October thaw had set in, Mirski and others like him were released from jails and told that their sentences were unjust, and that their trials had been rigged. They had known about it all along, but it was something new on the part of the State to admit it. They were offered formal rehabilitation trials, priority in employment and money to "compensate" for property that had been taken from them years before.

I had met with the group early that morning in the drafty emptiness of the Warsaw Municipal Court. Mirski's case—typical of thousands of similar cases now being tried all over Poland —was of special interest to me because at the time of the Warsaw uprising he had been in command of the sector in which my brother had fought. Ian had served as a courier between the Mokotowska Street unit and the Central Headquarters in midtown Warsaw. Sent on a vital assignment at the very height of the battle, he managed to make his way through the gruesome network of sewers only to be hit by a piece of German shrapnel at short range. Mirski did not witness Ian's death, but he remembered him well. "I can still see him," he said, while we sat on the long, marble bench, waiting for the doors to the courtroom to open, "a tall, slender boy of eighteen, with wavy golden blond hair and eyes framed by absurdly long, curly lashes. He was gay and seemingly unaware of the danger; even when covered with grime, he looked more like a well-brought-up college boy than a fighter."

Ian would have been thirty-one next July, I reflected; he too would probably have been punished for carrying out his duty as a Pole.

Teresa, Kazik's sister, sat next to me on the bench. She was small, dark-eyed and intense.

"The scene looks quite different from last time," she confided. "Kazik's first trial took place six years ago in this building, in the room right across from this hall. He was arrested early in 1949 and was held in jail for two years before we learned the nature of the charges against him. The prison was only three blocks away from here; but on the day of the trial the road was lined deep with military police on both sides, and a huge armored tank rumbled right behind the old car in which Kazik and his escort were riding. A machine gun was installed in the corner of the courtroom, and armored guards stood watch over the entrance to prevent the prisoner from escaping."

"Those were unnecessary precautions," laughed Kazik. "I was wracked by dysentery and was hardly able to stand up on my own. I lost twenty-three pounds in that jail."

"Were you allowed books or magazines?" I asked him.

"No, but I was allowed to play chess. I spent weeks teaching the game to my cellmate, and we used to go on playing for hours. Chess saved my sanity in those days," he added with a rueful expression.

Kazik Mirski was nineteen when, early in 1940, he first joined the underground network in German-occupied Poland. By 1944 he had become a veteran soldier, trained in the ways of sabotage and an expert at handling arms of all kinds. His chain of command led straight to the Polish Emigré Government in London, whose orders the vast underground state carried out. In those days Poland was the only occupied country in the world where the resistance movement took on the form of a factual underground government, with ministries, territorial administration, a parliament holding regular sessions, a secret education system, an army of over 300,000 men organized in regiments and divisions; there even were underground courts which administered justice "in the name of the President of the Polish Republic." Constant wireless contact was maintained with England, and arms and instructions were dropped by RAF planes over Poland in secret nocturnal rendezvous.

In July 1944 the Germans were falling back before the Russian advance in Poland. Patton's forces were sweeping through central France; it looked as if the end of the war was in sight. By the end of July the Russian armies under Marshal Rokossovsky came to the outer suburbs of Praga, barely six miles from the center of Warsaw. Russian planes passed over the city every day from bases only twenty miles distant.

In Warsaw the Polish underground waited. The Commander of the Polish Home Army, General Bor, was convinced that the Russians would begin their attack on the city almost immediately. Although he had never been able to establish direct contact with Rokossovsky, his radio picked up an appeal from Moscow for immediate armed action:

> "Poles, the time of liberation is at hand! Poles to arms! Make every Polish home a stronghold in the fight against the invader! There is not a moment to lose!"

The appeal was signed by Molotov, the Soviet Minister for Foreign Affairs, and Osobka-Morawski, the Moscow-made head of the "Committee of National Liberation," which called itself "the provisional Government of Poland." Similar Russian appeals were monitored in London that week; they all urged the Poles to rise against the Germans and to assist the Russian armies to cross the Vistula and enter Warsaw.

General Bor had deferred action for months. He knew that his forty thousand men would probably succeed in initially wresting the control of the city from the Germans, but he also was aware of the fact that they had just barely enough food and arms to last for seven days—and no more—if help from outside did not come.

The appeal, however, seemed clear. It was heard both in Warsaw and in London. A Red Army move to encircle Warsaw from the north seemed to be under way. It looked like the logical moment to strike.

General Bor did not have much experience with Russian duplicity. "There could be no purpose in inciting the people to an action which, if unsupported, would surely spell their slaughter," he notices in his memoirs.

By his failure to understand the Russian objective of that moment and the ruthless mechanics of the game of world politics, General Bor badly misjudged the situation and inflicted intolerable suffering on thousands of his compatriots.

The Home Army was ordered to come out of hiding and to attack at 5 P.M. on August 1, 1944.

What followed was tragedy.

Although the unexpected attack succeeded in liberating the city for a while, the Germans struck back savagely with tanks against the defenders' hand weapons. For two months a column of fire and smoke more than half a mile tall stood over the fighting city. British airmen flew long, murderously dangerous missions from distant Italian bases to drop supplies of arms to the insurgents, while well-equipped Soviet armies sat on the opposite bank of the Vistula sunbathing and waiting for Warsaw to die. The U. S. Government appealed to Stalin to permit American bombers with fighter escorts to organize a shuttle operation between England and Soviet-held bases a dozen miles east of Warsaw. The Russians delayed their reply for a month. Finally permission was granted for one flight, which took place on September 18, 1944. The arrival of the powerful American bombers cheered the exhausted defenders, but by then the Germans were in command of the greater part of the city and most of the precious "drops" fell into enemy hands.

After sixty-three days of fighting, when food and arms were exhausted and more than 250,000 people had perished, with water wells all polluted and disease starting to spread, the Home Army surrendered. It was an important victory for the well-armed German giant, who proceeded to destroy the city, house by house. The patiently-waiting Russian giant watched him with passive contentment; the situation was very much to his liking.

In allowing Warsaw to die, the Russians were motivated

by logic. Europe's postwar political pattern had already been designed by the Kremlin. In it Poland was to be Communist; a Polish puppet government had been in existence for some time, carrying out its functions under the protective umbrella of the Red Army. The well-organized underground state, loyal to the emigré "capitalist" government in London and supported by Russia's principal allies, was a powerful obstacle to the realizations of these plans. Why not let the large nucleus of the fanatically anti-Communist forces perish in self-inflicted destruction? Why help them? The only argument for help could have been human compassion. But compassion means little to Russia when compelling historical reasons are involved.

In the last days of the fighting Mirski was wounded. The injury was not serious, and he recovered his strength some weeks later.

"I used to wander around the rubble desert of Warsaw," he recalled, "unable to recognize even the most intimately familiar sights. In the dim light of a winter dusk the piled-up bricks, the gaping holes of the houses with their bits of personal possessions strewn around, the terrifying emptiness and the howling November wind seemed like an eerie landscape of the moon.

"Since most of the civilians had left Warsaw, I did not know where my parents and my sisters had gone," he went on. "I had not seen them since before the uprising and had no idea whether any of them had survived. The apartment house we lived in had been burned to the ground, so I went to live with friends in the suburbs, about fifteen miles out of Warsaw. Ten days later I ran into my mother on the street; she had returned and had been looking for me everywhere. For a few weeks we were all reunited in one spot, but then I was sent to Germany for forced labor. Luckily the end of the war came soon after, and I returned home in late spring."

"Not for long," interrupted his sister. "Three years later you went back into jail, to atone for having been a good Pole."

"How old are you now?" I asked Kazik.

"I am thirty-eight," he said smiling, "nearly forty. But since I have spent more than eleven years of my life in one political jail or another, I should say that I am almost sixty."

His smile was young and engaging.

A tall, bulky man with a large sheaf of papers came toward us hurriedly. "Get ready," he said to Kazik. "The judge has just arrived in his chambers. Your case is coming up any moment."

We all filed into the large, empty courtroom and took our seats near the window.

The court clerk read the text of the 1951 prison sentence, and Kazik's lawyer moved for striking it out of the record. The prosecutor announced that the State was withdrawing its charges. At his lawyer's request, Kazik told the Court the history of the last eighteen years of his life—an impassionate narrative of months of underground work, years spent in German prisons, escapes, a steady succession of perilous assignments—always in the service of Poland—the Communist persecution and the last six years spent in jail for alleged "treason" to Poland.

The judge sat motionless in his chair, but his eyes, steadily fixed on the defendant, were kind. He had listened to many similar cases, and they had never failed to move him. Compassion was evident on his face. Eighteen years in a man's life is a very long stretch—particularly if that man is thirty-eight years of age and has to begin his life all over.

After the court had recessed, the verdict was read by the clerk. The 1951 sentence for treason was annulled and struck out of Warsaw's municipal records. A sum of 35,000 zlotys ($1,500 at the official rate and about $325 at the actual rate) would be given to Kazik as compensation for "the unjust treatment he had been subjected to."

"What are your plans for the future?" I asked Kazik, after we had all left the court building and settled down in a *kawiarnia* on the square.

"Architecture, of course," he said smiling. "I am going to pick up where I left off when World War II interrupted my studies. I shall get a job on the side, and the 'dowry' I acquired should be helpful. I shall have to hurry to catch up with the world—and with life."

I left them to the gay babble of the *kawiarnia* and the quantities of cream puffs consumed eagerly all around.

A poster on a house in the Krakowskie Przedmiescie caught my eye. It listed the entries in the current competition for design of a monument to honor the heroes of the Warsaw uprising. Spontaneous public subscription, which had spread like wildfire throughout Poland, had raised the money for it.

"The wheel has turned a full circle," I remarked to myself, and walked on, thinking of Ian, my young brother.

CHAPTER 15

The Return of a Slave Laborer

"Moskwa-brzesc" read the notice on the long-distance express train, which pulled into the station at 8:30 a.m. sharp. Suddenly the deserted, ramshackle building became jam-packed with people. Scattered in small groups along the length of the platform, they were feverishly unloading and sorting out their possessions. It was an odd baggage: wooden boxes painted brown and dark red to make them look like suitcases, sagging cartons tied with odd pieces of string, burlap sacks packed with clothing, pots and pans, folding beds, old mattresses, dirty pillows, chairs with insides half torn out.

The new arrivals clung to these miserable belongings, guarding them jealously like a treasure. They looked for all the world like shipwrecks washed out on a shore by the waves. A man in a worn sheepskin coat, holding a small boy by the hand, stood guard over a cart piled with baggage. "We have been traveling for eleven days," I heard him say to a Red Cross worker on the platform. His eyelids were circled with red and he swayed a little as he talked. His wife sat on a wooden stool next to him, looking around apathetically, too tired to register emotion. Others were huddled together in small groups—indifferent, apprehensive and bewildered. This was a quiet homecoming, the return to Poland of people who had been deported from the eastern part of the country, when it was seized by Stalin in 1939. They were now arriving each day at points along the Polish-Soviet border. Close to five hundred thousand were expected to return; over a million and a half had been taken. Many were gone as long as sixteen years; tens of thousands of others are lost and will never be heard from again.

Two bare little rooms in the station have been converted into a reception center. A primitive coal-burning stove warmed a small part of the first room, in which at least twenty people were crowded. The wooden table was covered with sheets of paper bearing long lists of names.

"Name, place of birth—and where in Russia were you?" asked the Red Cross worker who sat behind the table, conducting the registration. The woman who stood before her was in her early thirties, but looked fifty. Her face was rough, weather-beaten, her hair grayish under a dark-colored kerchief. She was wearing an overcoat made of blankets and a pair of man's shoes laced with twine, a man's shirt and a skirt made of a cheap dark red cloth. Her name was Halina; her father used to be a professor of chemistry at the University of Lwow—the picturesque old city in Eastern Poland which is now part of Russia. She was only sixteen on that snowy January morning when the NKVD (Russian secret police) knocked at the door of the comfortable two-story house where she and her family had been living. The time was 5 A.M. and the sky outside was still dark. Her father opened the door.

"Get up and get ready," said the Russians. "Your number has come up; you are leaving."

Halina will never forget the horror on her mother's face as she turned to stare at her husband.

"Take warm things," the Russians advised cynically.

They were allowed one suitcase apiece. Halina put on her school dress, a pair of ski pants over it, the warmest jacket in her closet and grabbed a book of poems by Mickiewicz. The warmth of the white porcelain stove was the last thing she remembered of the house.

They walked out into the sting of the January winter, painfully trudging along to the station. Other groups met with them in the darkness, equally bewildered and scared. The long train was made up of cars that were used to transport cattle across Poland. They had not been cleaned from last use. Each car had two open holes, barred with wire, big enough for a cow to peer through. Heavy locks barred the exit. This was just one of the hundreds of similar trains that were soon to start moving east. Filled to capacity, the transport slowly moved out of the Lwow railroad station. Its destination was the Altai region in Central Asia—a great, bare desert land, where even a thousand miles is no distance. Summers in that part of the world are cruelly, blisteringly hot—the winters are long, dark and severe.

After a nightmarish journey of three weeks, during which the train discharged passengers many times, the family were dumped in the middle of a steppe, two miles from a collective farm. "You'll have to learn how to be useful," they were told.

Halina spent the next sixteen years of her life as a slave. She carried water from a well, chopped wood, worked long hours and was always, continuously, hungry. An additional piece of bread, an unused piece of string assumed the big, overwhelming importance of her life. Lwow, with its wide, tree-lined streets, lovely parks, gay *kawiarnias*, Roman churches and the laughing countryside around it took up the haziness of a dream. The enormous vastness of the steppes made all thought of escape seem absurd.

Unused to physical labor, her delicately beautiful mother died the first year from exhaustion, after carrying loads of turf on her back for five months. Shortly after, her father was sent to a distant farm to drive tractors. That was the last time she saw him.

Halina lived among people whose level of civilization was as low as that of the first inhabitants of this earth. They were not unkind or inhuman—they were simply savages without any knowledge of hygiene or health rules. She is one of the few who returned. The news of the repatriation program luckily seeped through the grapevine to her *kolkhoz*, and she managed to hitch onto a transport going west. Thousands of others like her are still slaving. Some have married or were compelled into marriage with a Russian; they bore children and will go through their miserable lives resenting the bitter injustice of their fate. Gradually their memories will grow dimmer, pushed aside by the daily effort to survive. Their children, who will speak Russian only, will remember a vague phrase or a song that their mother in a rare moment had taught them. One day they'll realize that "somehow she was different" from the local women around them.

I looked at Halina's ravaged face. She was bent over a Red Cross questionnaire, filling it with her unformed, childlike writing. She held the pencil awkwardly and her face was closed in like a mask. "Did she have any family left in Poland?" ran one question. None—except a few vague relatives, who also had been sent to Russia and are now being resettled in the west. She may join them or just "look around for a job"—perhaps in a factory, for a change. She was glad to be back, she remarked—at least, she will be among her own people.

She moved on into the adjoining room, where she was to

be examined by a doctor and given the standard repatriate's cash advance of 1,000 zlotys ($42 at the official rate) and some clothing. Others took her place in the line; more than a hundred people had arrived on the train.

There were farmers and doctors, lawyers, shopkeepers, factory workers and peasants, deported when entire villages were moved east. There were women with children born out of wedlock on the steppes and men who at twenty-five looked like sixty. Poorly clothed, undernourished—they all wore the same vacant expression on their faces. Of the horrors they went through, none would talk. The uncertain future ahead left them indifferent and resigned; nothing ever could be as bad as their past. These people had all been productive and law-abiding citizens in their days—still they had been swept away and destroyed because their existence in those lands ran contrary to the Soviet desire to push westward. Now they were being returned, following Gomulka's agreement with the Russians. They'd been picked up at random and sent west, asked to start a new life—and forget. But how can sixteen years of a life be erased from one's memory? How can one's wasted youth be replaced? How can a hopelessly mutilated life be salvaged and made to sustain itself once again? There is no compensation for such things; a crime has been committed, and the entire world knows who did it.

Why do the Poles hate the Russians? people ask. Why have they always hated them? The answer was right there in that room. The bedraggled people who stood there, still swaying from the subhuman existence they had led, were the victims of a Communist scheme for world conquest. But their forebears had suffered just as much from the tsars all throughout the 19th century and later up to World War I. Wave after wave of Poles were deported to Siberia in chains. Most were political prisoners who had plotted how to regain freedom from the tsars. Those were sent in "kibitkas," a rectangular box mounted on sleighs, big enough to stand in but not large enough to lie in, drawn by a pair of fast horses. The prisoner was chained to one side of the box and made to stand up inside it. The journey from Poland to a place inside Russia sometimes took two or three months. Horses and drivers were relayed every day; the prisoner was fed, but was never allowed to lie down. If he died, his body was thrown out and left in the wilderness.

"In deep snow, through an endless, flat countryside
Flies the kibitka; like the wind in a desert. . . ."

ran the poem we used to recite in our youth.

Such were the ways of justice of the tsars. Stalin's methods were even more thorough, and he had the modern means of communication at his disposal. The result was an ocean of human suffering.

The people who were brought to Brzesc on this train had lived in the old historical part of Poland which I loved. It was the old battleground between the East and the West across which hordes of Tartars had swept into Poland. The towns in that part of the world were still surrounded by high walls, and local songs told of battles waged by the Commonwealth of Poland against the Cossacks and the Turks. East of Lwow stretched the rolling plains of Podolia, a high plateau bound by a line of escarpments in the north. The soil there is black and rich, like the black earth of the Russian Ukraine. It produces magnificent crops of wheat, hemp and tobacco. The rivers flow in deep canyon-like valleys called "yary," where lush fruit and vegetables are grown. There is an open prairielike magnificence to the landscape. Small villages nestle cozily against the deep sides of the yary, dominated by the onion-shaped domes of the churches.

This was the land of the Arab horses and of the big, feudal estates which ran into thousands and thousands of acres. Sometimes driving across a wild country, one would come across an oak grove, or a forest; the birch, the oak and the alder would suddenly open wide, and a graceful 18th-century house would appear from nowhere, or a château built by Italian craftsmen way back in the 16th century. There would be carefully tended grounds, tennis courts, swimming pools, miles of macadam highway to the station, French and English periodicals and recent models of cars in the garages. There would be hospitals and grade schools maintained by the local landowner at his expense, recreation halls and child centers for the people who worked on his land: a cohesive, secure little unit, run in a patriarchal style—feudal, yet rich in tradition and serene.

I remember visiting with my father in Podhorce—a handsome castle of white stone, with a moat, an Italian courtyard and a lovely sweeping view of the country. It was summer; we were standing on the terrace before dinner, looking east toward Russia, which was close, barely twenty-five miles away. Below us lay the village—picturesque and pin-neat, resting in the shadow of the "big house"; toward the horizon beyond stretched rich fields in high cultivation. The Polish flag flew proudly from the small post office in the distance.

"This," said my father, "is a salient, an outpost of Western culture farthest east. For six hundred years it has been a part of the West—it will be a sad day when it goes."

Not having been to Poland since prewar, I found it difficult to remember how much the frontiers had been shifted. Here I was in the Brzesc railroad station, looking east, straight toward the Polesie marshes, which though close were not a part of Poland any more. I wanted to revisit the town of Pinsk—"the capital of the marshes"—which I used to know in my childhood. But I couldn't. I could only wistfully remember the old days.

Polesie, the "land of the marshes," was the most sparsely

populated part of Poland. A large province, drained by the
river Prypec, a tributary of the Dnieper, it was a region of
ancient settlement, but man had not been able to modify its
landscape.

What I remember best of Polesie is its silence—the great,
solemn silence of the marshes. It was broken only now and
then by the swish of a canoe paddle—the only means of transportation in those parts. The silence of nature extended to the
inhabitants of the marshes. Quietly, with an unerring instinct,
they poled their flat-bottomed boats through miles of un-
charted waterways. They seldom sang or talked loudly. They
were a hardy lot—resourceful and self-sufficient. For generations they had known no other horizon but these marshes.
They loved them and seldom went any distance away. That
was until the deportations began.

The town of Pinsk was the rallying point for the province.
It lay across the old land route between the Baltic and the
Black seas, known as the "amber road" of antiquity. Since
time immemorial, Baltic amber used to be a vital article of
trade with Byzantium, and then with the Turkish Ottoman
Empire, which replaced it. In the 18th century a canal was
cut across the waterways of Polesie to connect the marshes
with the Vistula River; timber and tar were shipped from the
province into the interior of Poland, and Pinsk acquired a
position of importance.

Market day in prewar Pinsk was a memorable occasion.
The usually quiet waterfront alongside the old Jesuit Church
was filled with boats of all sizes; everything came to the market by boat. There were dozens of geese stacked in heaps,
with feet tied so they could not get away; fish of all kind,
sold directly from boats; mushrooms, of which there were
quantities in the woods; willow baskets, marsh grass, hay sold
by the wagonload on dry land, lumber, birch logs, wood for
shingles, earthenware and large quantities of firewood. Farm-

ers who brought large hogs or live calves arrived at the market in horse wagons, taking the longer, circular land route. One saw peasants carrying live sheep on their backs. Men and women wore clothes of homespun linen or wool. The men's hats were made of black sheepskin, and most of them wore birch-bark sandals and cloth leg wrappings instead of socks. (They were called *powijaki* and were deemed more practical than socks.) Only the comparatively well off could afford leather boots. I remember the delicious-tasting wild mushrooms fried in butter, sold at the market food stands, and the crowded cafés filled with people consuming quantities of beer and of the potato-distilled local vodka. At sunset the market came to an end. Long lines of carts jammed the only highway out of town. The flat-bottomed boats, now empty, left the waterfront near the church. After a day of fête, the Polesie peasant would resume his solitary existence in the marshes.

Pinsk was now in a different world, separated from the old country by a frontier. Did they have any more market days? No one knew. Polesie was not Poland any more. Its people had been shifted west or deported. I remember a village near Kosow, at the northern tip of the marshes, with the impossible name of Mereczowszczysna—we used to dare our foreign friends to pronounce it—that was the birthplace of Tadeusz Kosciuszko, the Polish national hero who fought in the American Revolution. The attractive one-story house with a white colonnaded verandah used to be carefully preserved as a shrine. Now it is on the wrong side of the border and is slowly falling apart from neglect.

The sky in the east had turned dark. A blanket of fog came between me and the marshes. I turned round and walked back to the station where the return train to Warsaw was now waiting.

I saw many of the repatriates on this train. They were si-

lent, too tired or too apathetic to talk. Some were going to
meet relatives in Warsaw; others were off to Legnica in the
west, where they would be resettled and assigned jobs. The
so-called "recovered territories," which were going to be
their home from now on, used to be a part of East Germany
which in the postwar shift of frontiers had come under Polish
administration. Way back in the 14th century they were
Polish, but for the last six hundred years they had been inhabited by the Germans. Poland now claimed them as their
own, but no final settlement with the Germans had been
made. How permanent was the new settlers' future? No one
knew.

When the train came into the Warsaw station, the repatriates waited for everybody else to get off. They then proceeded to unload their belongings, checking each miserable
sack carefully. Volunteers from among Warsaw students appeared on the platform to meet them. I turned back to see
whether they had finally come to life, but there was the same
vacant expression on their faces.

CHAPTER 16

The Recovered Territories

"DEAR KRYSIA," said the postcard that I found at the Bristol Hotel the same night, "I hear that you are planning a visit to the 'recovered territories' in the West. I have been stationed there for a long time and could help you to make a plan of what to see. I also would like to see *you*."

The postcard was signed "Yurek."

Yurek was a younger cousin of mine, who often spent summers with us in the country because his family lived in Warsaw. He must have been about seven or eight years younger than I was, so I never paid much attention to him in those days. All I remembered was a blue-eyed, blond little boy in knee pants who used to follow my brother everywhere and was being mercilessly bossed by him; he never learned how to ride a pony properly, but was good at swimming and sailing boats. I had heard that he had joined the Polish Army as a regular officer, had been sent to the Military Academy in Moscow for training and had returned with the rank of a major, and a job on the General Staff. I remember how annoyed I had felt at the news that he had gone to Moscow to study; I put a black mark on his record and promptly forgot all about him.

Now I was curious to see what sort of person he was and

where he stood with relation to the post-October changes. "May I come straight up to your room?" he inquired, when I called him and asked whether we could meet the next day. "The downstairs lobby at the Bristol is a madhouse and we would not recognize each other in the crowd."

I was glad, for it meant that the freedom to talk to outsiders had seeped through the ranks of the Army.

Yurek was now a tall, thin young man in his late twenties, with a receding hairline, large blue eyes and the same slow, happy grin of his boyhood. He came dressed in a navy-blue business suit. "My uniform after duty," he called it. First he shook my hand solemnly, then laughed and embraced me with affection. We had tea and talked for a long time. It was fun to remember the old days—the house and the games in the park—and how he and my brother Ian got spanked when they put two enormous bullfrogs in our old French governess's bed, which scared her out of her wits.

"Yurek," I said, "I must tell you I was furious when I heard that you had gone to Moscow to study. I was afraid that perhaps you had turned Communist. Why on earth did you have to go there?"

He looked astonished and hurt. Then he smiled in his slow, pleasant way. "I am a professional soldier," he said, "and I want to learn all I can. In those day the only place I could study was in Russia. I spent a nightmarish three years but I learned about the military art all right. Someday Poland will profit from my knowledge."

"Were you chosen," I asked, "or did you apply to go there?"

"I was among the top five of my class," he said, "so the opportunity was offered, and I took it. There was an additional reason for my move. As you know, I had to support my mother, who was suffering from a complicated malady of the liver. She needed expensive drugs and good care. From

Moscow I could send her large packages each week duty free and all the medicines that she needed. Thanks to this, the last two years of her life were made peaceful."

I remembered Aunt Maia as I knew her, a gay, dark and vivacious small woman, with a great talent for painting, which she never had the chance to develop. She had a passion for walking, and I used to accompany her on endless excursions in the fields.

"Where were you when October burst out?" I asked Yurek.

"I was right here in Rembertow, near Warsaw," he said. "The Military Academy was astir. We stayed up all through the night declaring our support for Gomulka. Next day not one Russian officer or instructor was left. We sent them packing rather rudely, but they knew how we resented their presence."

"Did you know Rokossovsky?" I asked.

"Yes, I worked under his command for a year. He is a top professional soldier, one of the great military commanders of our day—a strange man, taciturn and aloof, with a mixed-up tragic past. You know," he said, lighting an American cigarette I gave him, "we all hated Rokossovsky's name and his presence. We looked at him as the symbol of Russian domination, as Stalin's watchdog and as a Muscovite superimposed on us against our will. The fact that he had been born in Poland, spoke Polish and even behaved like a Pole made our dislike of him even worse. Now that more about him has become known, he reminds me of a figure out of a Greek tragedy. Curiously, he has never belonged anywhere; something like a curse seems to have dominated his life. It is a fascinating story. One day someone will write a book about it. As an old-time Communist and a Pole, in spite of his Russian upbringing, he was fond of Warsaw, his birthplace; yet each time he attempted to return, his return spelled misfortune to

the country, and he was greeted with hatred and resentment.
Suspect as a Communist—because of his Polish origin—he was
thrown into a concentration camp by Stalin in 1937; then he
was hastily brought back in 1941 to take over the defense of
Stalingrad and Moscow. His dislike of the satrap in the Kremlin was intense, yet it was as a symbol of Stalinism that he had
to leave Poland in disgrace. In Russia he was looked at with
suspicion as a Pole, yet his own city and country rejected
him as a traitor. A curious irony of fate has dodged his footsteps all his life. In August of 1944 he was in command of
the Soviet Army which reached the Vistula, then stopped at
the suburbs of Warsaw. For two months he watched the
Polish Home Army's fight against the German Wehrmacht
and received their desperate appeals for help. It lay in his
power to save Warsaw: he could have entered his native city
as a triumphant liberator, but he never ordered his tanks to
move forward. Stalin forbade him to do so—his orders were
clear and precise—and as a Russian general he felt he could
not disregard them. Naturally, the insurgents believed that
he had deliberately waited to allow the Germans to destroy
them. When he finally entered Warsaw five months later, he
was greeted with universal hatred and told how thousands
had died cursing his name. The city was a mass of ruins, and
even the landmarks of his childhood were gone.

"We all resented his appointment as Polish Minister of Defense in 1949," Yurek went on. "We blamed him for the
presence of the Russian advisers in our midst. Actually, they
had been put there by Stalin way back in 1945, but we
thought Rokossovsky was responsible for their presence.
What we did not know in those days was that Stalin had
never trusted the Marshal. For the hero of Stalingrad to be
appointed Minister of Defense in a satellite government was
a comedown in prestige. To us, however, he was 'Stalin's man
of confidence,' and we hated his name and his face. It is now

being said that, thanks to his mitigating influence, the Polish Army has never been put into Russian uniforms, as Rakosi did in Hungary, and that he was wrongly held responsible for the movement of troops during the October change-over. In fact, it was Konew who ordered the Russian divisions to start in the direction of Warsaw. Still, public opinion in Poland will always blame Rokossovsky for it."

"Where is he now?" I asked.

"Oh, he is back in Russia, of course. He's been appointed Soviet Vice-Minister of Defense, to compensate for the humiliation that he has suffered in Poland. He is a man in his late fifties, and a long military career still lies ahead of him. He will go on serving Russia and try to forget the nemesis that has stood between him and the land of his birth."

We talked about the new commander-in-chief, General Marian Spychalski, a former architectural engineer who fought in the underground movement during the war and was in prison at the same time as Gomulka. A tall, good-looking man, with a fine, intellectual face, he has been described as "a nationalist in feeling, but Communist by profession."

Said Yurek: "He knows damn well that if the Soviets intervened, as they did in Hungary, the entire Polish Army would fight. I don't believe he would do anything to stop us. He also knows that we *would* go to war on the side of the Russians if the Germans tried to take away the territories that we have regained in the west. Our Army is now being reduced because the government is trying to cut down on expenses, but it's still a pretty efficient organization. It is said that it has two abiding hates: the Russians and our great German neighbor to the west."

"Which hate takes precedence?" I inquired.

Yurek laughed and got up to look out of the window in the darkness. "I should say that the Russians do, by a very considerable margin. But the shadow of Germany still looms big. Go to the western territories on the Oder, and you will understand why people there are afraid of tomorrow."

Among the books that we were made to read in our school-days was a historical novel called *Krzyzacy (The Knights of the Cross)*, by the popular Polish writer, Sienkiewicz. Painted against the background of 15th-century Europe, it is a fascinating account of the wars waged by the Polish people against the Teutonic Knights of Prussia.

The order of the Teutonic Knights was one of the three great military and religious orders that sprang from the Crusades. Its initial purpose was charity and care of the sick, but toward the beginning of the 13th century it had developed into a military club exercising rights of sovereignty and of conquest on the troubled confines of Christendom along the shores of the Baltic Sea. Poland was already Catholic—it was converted to Christianity as early as 966 A.D.—but the Prussian tribes to the north were still pagan, and so were Lithuania and the Baltic provinces to the east. In the year 1228—a sad date in Polish historical annals—Konrad, the Polish Duke of Masovia, invited the Teutonic Order to help him subdue the heathens of East Prussia. For the next two hundred years the Teutonic Knights ruthlessly spread the German rule eastward under the cover of a religious war. It was the beginning of the historical German "Drang nach Osten" which has ever since spelled danger to the existence of the Polish Slavs.

As time went on, lust for territorial expansion replaced the religious zeal of the Crusaders. As their military power increased, their war methods became more and more cruel. They attacked Christians and heathens alike, ransacked churches, robbed convents and religious orders. The specter of a Teutonic Knight dressed in armor, a huge black cross painted over his white Crusader's cloak, a rosary in one hand and a loaded gun in the other, haunted the terrified peoples of Northern Poland, Prussia and Lithuania for over two centuries. The Knights' headquarters were in Marienburg, a fortress-town in what is now Northern Poland. From there they made lightning forays into the countryside, burning towns, murdering people and taking hostages for whom they demanded gold ransom. After several unsuccessful attempts, the Knights were finally defeated by the Polish King Wladyslaw Jagiello in a battle at Grunwald in 1410—the last victory the Poles ever won over the Germans. Their military power was broken; they had to surrender their lands and withdraw. But the legend of the Teutonic Knights handed down in songs and in ballads still lives on the western frontiers of Poland.

"Will the Germans come back?" asked Bronislaw Yankowski, a farmer from a village near Lwow, who had just been resettled near Wroclaw (formerly Breslau) in Poland's "recovered territories." He and his wife and two girls were pleased with their new piece of land. They worked hard and hoped that the farm would soon start paying off. The house they lived in was better than the one they had owned in the east; it was a solid, two-story brick structure with electricity and running water. The prospects for the future were good, but Bronislaw felt insecure and uncertain; he was troubled by the memory of the former owner of the farm; he feared that someday the German would be coming back.

The Oder-Neisse lands, the so-called recovered territories, which in 1945 the Soviet Union had carved out of East Germany and handed over to Poland in exchange for Eastern Poland they annexed, make up about one-third of present-day Poland. Eight million Germans have left the area, and more than six million Poles have moved in as new settlers—a shift of population achieved at a cost of immense human suffering. Now, for the first time in six hundred years, the entire area

is inhabited by Poles. It is a *fait accompli* which nothing in
the future can change. There is hardly a Pole—no matter what
his political opinion—who would question that these territories
should be anything but Polish. None of the Western powers
has recognized the adjustment, and there is no German agreement on the frontier. On the contrary, the expelled Germans
yearn to return to their homes. Surrounded by strong feelings
on both sides, these lands remain an explosive bone of con-
tention. In the meantime the Poles are firmly in possession
and are prepared to fight to maintain the present status quo
on the Oder. It is a part of the devilish Russian game that
the Red Army should remain the only guarantee the Poles
have to confirm their title to these lands.

Ruins and desolation—and gnawing uncertainty for the future: this was the overwhelming impression I got from my
trip across the Oder and Neisse lands. Nowhere are the fantastic results of Communist mismanagement more obvious
than in this beautiful countryside of birch forests, wide rivers
and smiling little towns with red roofs, an area which used to
be one of the most prosperous corners of Central Europe.
Twelve years after the end of the war, town after town lies
in ruins. Mud flows across the cobbled streets, skeletons of
once-graceful houses stand sadly in need of rebuilding. The
small private industry, which once was the mainstay of the
region, has slowly become extinct under the pressure of senseless nationalization and confiscatory taxes. People have moved
away from the towns since there was no work and no future.
Now farmers are coming back to the land, but the towns are
still deserted and ghostlike. The few remaining Germans
who had stayed are now leaving for West Germany when
they can.

Only the industrial complex of Upper Silesia, the Polish
Ruhr, where one city merges into the next for over 25 miles,
remains a bustling area of its own. The Silesian coal mines,

steel mills and chemical plants are the most valuable assets
the Poles received from the Germans. Poland now possesses
the basic essentials to become one of the important industrial
nations in Europe. But they must first free themselves from
the shackles of doctrinaire State-socialism which hampers individual progress and makes Western technical help ineffec-
tive.

More and more repatriates from the east are being resettled on the Oder. With more elastic economic policies since
October, the desolated areas may soon begin to take on a new
life. The Poles lack German efficiency, so the rebuilding
process will be slow. But the uncertainty for the future still
remains, haunting the new settlers like a ghost.

"Will the German in whose house I am living return and
demand restitution?" women like Halina keep asking. After
sixteen years of slave labor they yearn for security and for
peace. Will they ever get it? No one knows.

Between the constant Russian drive westward and the traditional German push to the east, the defiantly nationalistic
Poles are left uncomfortably insecure. Their strength is the
tenacious tradition of a tough and irrepressible people, who
after a thousand years of tempestuous history have managed
to emerge more vital and more nationalistic than before—in
spite of geography, which has been Poland's curse through
the ages.

CHAPTER 17

The Joys of Bureaucracy

ONE of the multiple reasons why life in a Communist country can never be lived pleasantly is that its normal functioning is made almost impossible by the vast armies of people unnecessarily employed at all levels. In Poland's planned economy, efficiency is not considered important. What matters is full employment. Labor productivity is low, because the incentives are few; firing for absenteeism is unheard of; the salaries are small—there has to be enough money to go round.

The girl at the hotel switchboard gets tired of connecting the calls. She works eight hours a day at a salary of about $75 a month. With meat at ninety-five cents a pound and butter at over a dollar—if and when she can get it—her wages are barely enough to feed her. She lives in a room with four people and dislikes to go back there at night. She owns a skirt, two or three blouses, a few scarves. What she really longs for is a good lipstick, a pair of American nylons and face creams; but those are not available except at black-market prices. She does not know her job well, because nobody took the trouble to train her. Though the number of telephone operators is triple that which a large American hotel would require, there is not one professional among them. Nobody gives a damn—not even the supervisor, whose job is equal

229

in prestige to that of a factory foreman. So, with alarming frequency it is decided now and then that all the hotel guests are out for a while. Calls come streaming in, but the exasperated caller is told, "There is no answer from the room." So you die of frustration awaiting the call that won't come. After a week or two one learns. A helpful friend or colleague suggests: "Go down and talk to the switchboard. Get acquainted; tell them that *all* your calls are important." It helps—and they make a supreme effort to relay at least one out of four messages. As I found out for myself, they are good girls; it is the system that is wrong.

During my stay in Warsaw I watched an American news-paperman complain to assembled room clerks at the Bristol that he had found two cables addressed to him in somebody else's box. They had been laying there for three days. "Don't you understand," he said, trying hard to control his exaspera-tion, "that a cable is *always* important. My newspaper may be telling me to go to another country tomorrow. I may get into trouble for not answering immediately."

"We understand very well," said the pleasant bosomy head clerk looking sternly at her all-too-numerous assistants. "Such mishaps will no longer happen, I assure you. We shall check all the mailboxes every day. Here you are," she said eagerly. "Just arrived." And she handed him a large envelope ad-dressed to a man who lived in a room next to him.

I had many meals at the Bristol and in other State-owned restaurants, since there were few private ones at the time. I learned to know the faces and the names of the waiters, but there was one stratagem I have never been able to catch on to. It was that of "Kolega." ("Kolega" in Polish means "col-league.") This is the way it worked: One sat down at a table and tried to order a meal. There were always plenty of waiters around—three or four usually hovered within a short distance from my table—and they did not seem to be busy.

I turned, waved and said several times, *"Prosze pana"* (Please, sir); this is the way in which all waiters in countries of the "socialist bloc" prefer to be addressed. Finally one would come with a menu, and I would quickly choose something. But before I had time to order anything on the menu, the waiter would disappear with a murmured "Kolega." I would find myself in the void. What he was trying to tell me was that he was "just going off duty," or that my table was not within his daily allotment, or simply that he was tiring of serving—his "kolega" would be along in a moment. Sometimes the "kolega" appeared and stayed with one until coffee; sometimes he left one in midstream at the meat course, in which case one had to start all over again. All "kolegas" agree that presenting the check is a nuisance that should be delayed forever. Tips in a Communist country are frowned on; only the foreigners give them, so what is there as incentive? The restaurant belongs to the State, a distant anonymous employer—the salaries are small and are likely to remain so in the future. Why work? Why be efficient? For whom? No one will fire you anyway!

The breakfast of Shepard Stone became a *cause célèbre* at the Bristol.

Mr. Stone, Director of the International Affairs Program of the Ford Foundation, had just arrived in Warsaw to work out the details of the exchange of students under the half-million-dollar Ford Foundation grant. He was a busy man, conducting interviews from early morning until night. He left precise instructions to have breakfast brought into his room every morning at eight o'clock. It arrived at a quarter to eight the first morning; next day it came at seven-fifteen and got him out of bed in a hurry; the day after, he waited frustrated, until a cheerful waiter knocked at his door after nine.

"It was just one of those mornings," he recalled, "when it

was impossible to start even thinking without breakfast."

"What's the matter, why don't you follow a routine?" he asked the jovial and pleasant waiter, who looked at him in amazement.

"I am only one hour late. That's not much. You are not catching a plane, are you?" the waiter asked.

No, he wasn't. And he ceased to care finally. It was just as well, because in the next two weeks he got his breakfast on time only once!

The genial lunacy of the waiters—most of them pleasant and very cheerful fellows—sometimes leads to unexpected results. Once, in Krakow, I came down in the morning to find several newspaper people I knew just finishing their coffee and rolls. They told me that they had ordered an omelette, but that as there were no signs of its ever arriving they had contented themselves with coffee and rolls. I, too, ordered coffee and rolls. The others departed.

I sat there for a good half hour, getting hungrier and angrier by the minute. Then a waiter appeared, one huge smile. He was carrying triumphantly the largest omelette I have ever seen, about two feet in length and ten inches wide. He set it proudly before me on the bare table: an omelette had once been ordered; an omelette had now arrived. I told him to take it back to the kitchen and quickly ran away from the monster.

The Polish airline LOT—a monopoly of the State—carries about thirty-six thousand passengers in a year and operates services as far away as Cairo. It employs over a thousand people—the exact figure is a State secret. Their pilots are excellent, and so is their safety record, in spite of the rather dilapidated machines that they fly. There are some very good people in LOT, particularly in the Overseas Branch, but their work is constantly handicapped by countless duds, who should never have been employed in a white-collar capacity.

"I have been asking this lady to stay home, not to work," one of the LOT employees told me. "I promised to see to it that her salary be continued until she is ready to retire. But she insists on arriving punctually at 8 A.M. every day. She does not like to stay home—I don't blame her—living conditions are bad; but once she is at the office I can't stop her from answering inquiries, and she usually answers them incorrectly. Well, nobody cares, anyway." He shrugged his shoulders discouragedly.

I *did* care—quite a lot. For three days I had been trying to get a ticket rerouted and advance reservations to Paris confirmed. It was a simple, routine matter, but the lady official looked at me as if I had come from the moon.

"Now, now, please don't get impatient," my friend said, trying to soothe me with a smile. "It shall all be done eventually. This is not America, you know. We, too, will one day be efficient, but we shall have to fire our cadres first."

A telephone rang at his elbow. I recognized the voice of an American photographer I know. He was trying to get information about a Warsaw-Prague flight the same day.

"What a good thing you called!" the cheerful girl at the counter chirped into the receiver. "I was just thinking that perhaps we *should* have contacted you today. The plane you were taking this evening has been canceled. Did you know?"

Judging by the silence at the other end, he was stunned.

I went along with Yasia, a Polish girl friend of mine, to the Polish Savings Bank . . . to cash a check. The imposing edifice, with a marble hallway and yellow walls, was crowded with people. Long lines stood in front of each window. Yasia handed her check to a clerk who checked the signature carefully, then gave it to a second girl, who after looking at it some more gave it to a third one, who checked the account and registered the amount of the check; the fourth clerk checked the new balance, and finally the cashier, or fifth clerk, paid out the sum, equivalent to about ten dollars. The operation took well over twenty minutes. I could not help comparing it with the two minutes it usually takes to cash a check anywhere in the United States. I reflected on the astronomic number of minutes and precious hours thus wasted by Polish citizens who cash checks or settle other matters with their banks.

Where does the difference lie? It is mostly a question of the organization of work and the willingness to do it from above.

I was told of a rule that existed in Polish Government offices before October—and was still being practiced in the provinces—which specified that no official should handle more than four to five business letters a day, no matter how short. The purpose of it was, of course, to provide enough work to go round for all the politically reliable know-nothings.

The rule does not exist any longer, but it is still pretty hard for an employer to fire a lower official or a worker simply because he refuses to work at his job.

While fighting for its economic life, the country is smothered with red tape. It has no concept of business administration, no continuity of business tradition and no desire for efficiency.

All moviehouses in Poland are owned and administered by the State. People frequently complain that there are too few of them in the country. "We can't afford to build new ones," says the State, but it is reluctant to admit that the cost of the bureaucratic machine created to administer the *kina* (cinemas) consumes millions of zlotys a year.

The socialist planners decide arbitrarily which film is going to be popular and where; they fix the number of showings in each town, predict cash receipts and attendance; the film schedules are rigid, according to the demands of the "Plan." In order to fulfill the "Plan," each cinema is supposed to show a given number of films in a year. It makes no difference whether the moviehouse in Poznan showing a French film with Fernandel is jammed to capacity; after the allotted number of days, the film is removed and sent on to Kielce or Radom in the provinces, where people care nothing about it. The public in Poznan is incensed because few had the chance to see Fernandel—but the moviehouse in Radom stands empty. It does not bother the officials in the slightest. The "Plan" is more important than the profits. Naturally, the State loses money by the million. Why does the senseless procedure keep on? Because the planners in Warsaw and their subordinates in the provinces would all be out of jobs if a businesslike system were adopted.

The Polish Socialist State has magnanimously assured its citizens of full medical care at no cost. All doctors are employees of the State; it owns all the hospitals and is the only authorized dispenser of medical drugs. But the general health of the country—compared to prewar days—is at an all-time low, and the medical standards are poor.

"We don't know which of the two immediate necessities is more pressing: new hospitals or new housing," a harassed Warsaw city official has told me. In Infant Jesus Hospital in Warsaw I saw X-ray apparatus glued together with tape, surgical instruments black with age and still used in the operating rooms. Few thermometers are available; one large hospital had only twelve of them to go round. I was told that in the obstetrical ward of a hospital in Wroclaw X-ray capsules were being inserted with bare hands because no money had been made available to purchase protective garments for the staff. In Stalin days any politically reliable student could embark on a nursing career, if she wished. As a result, some hospitals are staffed with young nurses fluent in political gibberish but with little elementary knowledge of medicine or hygiene. The old-timers had been dismissed or discouraged; a few are coming back, but not many.

There is a chronic shortage of drugs. Aureomycin, terramycin and chloromycetin can only be bought on the black market. Around the middle of each month State pharmacies regularly run out of penicillin. Fortunes have been made by selling U. S. or other foreign-obtained drugs on the black market. Distribution of the simplest medicines like cough syrups or vitamin preparations is hampered by lack of bottles and jars because the "estimate of consumption" forecast by the State's central planning ran about 40 percent below the needs of the pharmaceutical industry in the country.

In spite of the deplorable level of general health in the country, the amount of money allotted to the Ministry of Health is small compared to Propaganda or Planning. It ranks seventeenth—one of the last items on the list of the Commission for State's Economic Planning.

On a rainy day in late March I went with Anka, my energetic cousin and friend, to get medicine for her husband. Poor Gustaw had been suffering from a liver ailment and Anka, when I met her, was rushing to the pharmacy down the street. It had a large sign saying *Apteka*, and inside was what looked like a hopelessly long line of coughing, sneezing and obviously flu-ridden people. It was late afternoon. Outside the windows of the *Apteka* the little muddy square looked gray and forlorn. From time to time a new person would squeeze in through the door, his wet clothes steaming from the heat of the overcrowded room.

After nearly one hour's wait, we got to the head of the line. The harassed nurse, wearing a neat little white cap on her hair, examined the collection of papers in Anka's hands.

There was a slip of paper authorizing Anka to apply to the Regional Medical Board of her district for prescription; there was the prescription of her doctor, duly stamped and approved by the district's Medical Supervisor; there was the district's Pharmaceutical Department's authorization to issue cholesol—a new drug, certified by Warsaw's Pharmaceutical Council. I looked over Anka's shoulder and shuddered.

"How long did it take you to get this simple prescription?" I asked.

"About three days," said Anka. "I am lucky that the medicine is available. Sometimes they are out of one kind, but the pharmacy is not authorized to issue an alternative drug instead—even if the doctor himself lists it as second choice on the paper. One then has to start the entire routine from scratch."

The nurse finally decided that the papers were all in order. She handed us a slip to be presented to the cashier, where we obtained a fat bottle of pink liquid and a box of yellowish tablets.

The lunatic adherence to the "Plan" runs through all branches of Polish economic life. If a brand of cosmetics or a certain kind of raincoat fails to sell because of poor quality or other reasons, its production will continue nevertheless— because the Plan must be fulfilled. As a result, a store choked with merchandise that does not sell will go on receiving new supplies. On the other hand, constant shortages of the most common everyday items keep arising because planners had underestimated the demand. Want to buy a needle and a spool of thread? Impossible. The local State-owned department store has not had any for eight months. Want to have a tear darned in your suit? Be prepared for the local workmen's coöperative to keep it at least half a year.

Since October private initiative has been stepping into the
gap, but even during the darkest days of the Stalin regime
a little of it existed surreptitiously. One could always find
private tailors and shoemakers who worked "only for
friends"; plumbers willing to fix a water main in the house
of a neighbor who had been waiting for weeks for the local
State office to do it; doctors, dentists, private restaurants con-
cealed in somebody's house, and the like. Human nature cannot easily be changed, and the demand for private services will
never cease to exist.

Years of Communist exploitation have created economic
stagnation in Poland. One of its most direct results is a profound decline in social responsibility. Life is hard, so everyone
tries to fend for himself without regard for the common good
or communal discipline. The law of the jungle has become a
prevalent rule.

"In Poland everybody steals." I must have heard this phrase
hundreds and hundreds of times. It is not from one another
that they steal; common thefts are no more frequent than in
any other country—the State is the one that gets robbed.
Way back in the days of the war, when the Germans were
occupying Poland, people started to steal from the Germans;
it was then called "sabotage" and was thought patriotic. Communism set in next, and the State became the sole owner of
everything in the country. The result was general poverty.

So the State, which failed to provide its citizens with the
bare minimum to exist, gets robbed every day, every hour by
its resentful employers and their families. Most Poles have
come to accept it as a natural phenomenon. Workers in factories steal entire wagonloads of cement or of coal; they resell
them on the black market the same day. Salesgirls in State-
owned shops steal merchandise—anything from toilet paper
to shoes—and quickly resell it among friends. Tax collectors

CHAPTER 18

The New Generation

"**O**H GOD, make them play that tune again—now!" whispered Mariola, her eyes dreamy, face vibrant with concentrated excitement. The lilting notes of *As Time Goes By* floated across the arched, low-ceilinged room. The girl smiled at her companion and together they drifted toward the crowded dance floor. He was tall, thin, almost gawky, with straight features and blond hair carefully thrust to the back; she was lithe, dark haired, delicate, with enormous gray eyes which appeared even bigger in her smooth, finely chiselled little face. They seemed lost in a dream, as she softly hummed the Polish words of Bing Crosby's romantic song made popular in the war-time film *Casablanca*. The hour was close to 5 A.M. but the dance floor was as crowded as it had been in the early hours of the evening. Most of the young people around were drinking black coffee or *fruktovit*, a sugary concoction of soda water and synthetic orange juice; a few had vodka on their tables, but not many; music and dancing were the real stimulus. They would go on sitting there all night—talking, dancing and listening to music.

The tunes were old sentimental Polish tangos, slow-foxes and moody, war-time American jazz. No sheet music from abroad had been available for a long time so the orchestra played mostly by ear. In the early hours of the evening there had been some excited rock and roll; now the mood was romantic and subdued. An amazing concentration on the moment, combined with an effervescent champagne-like liveliness, radiated from the young couples in the room. They seemed to be totally oblivious to everything except the enjoyment of the brief, present moment of fun, intent on savoring every single second of it to the full.

> *"Our dreams are golden, our memories are brief,*
> *To-morrow's far, uncertain and . . . bewildering . . ."*

The catching words, the haunting melody matched the general mood to perfection. Not one face in the crowd was languid or blasé. A keen, sensitive awareness of life, an undercurrent of excitement made the room astir and pulsating.

This was a familiar atmosphere. I had come across it in cafés, where Poles gather for hours to talk politics and to argue, at students' balls during the recent carnival season in Warsaw, among the audience of a particularly good theatrical play or a concert, at gatherings in private homes, where everyone sits on the floor of one impossibly crowded little room, downing vodka, but where the real attraction is good talk. Always the same feeling of vitality, suppressed excitement, total, headlong immersion in the present, the connoisseur's delight in the brilliant game of conversational ping-pong. "Let's enjoy all this while we can," they seem to impart to each other, "for who knows what tomorrow will bring?" Danger is never far removed; it has been a constant in Polish everyday life through the years. It creates tension, but it also acts as a powerful intellectual stimulus, sharpens the senses and makes the exchange of thought lively and bubbling with high-spirited repartees. To many Poles it is a fair compensation for the lack of security and comfort.

The average Pole has never had too large a share of life's

blessings. Good talk, the company of friends are among the few available pleasures left to him. He attends to them lovingly and has managed to turn them into a very fine art. In Poland's classless society the real aristocrats today are the intelligentsia: writers, poets, philosophers, politicians, who have mastered the art of good conversation and good writing. They are lovingly followed, revered, and always outrageously praised. The road to such success is a hard one—satire and the art of debunking being the two favorite national pastimes—but once arrived at the top the writer, philosopher, and poet are securely enthroned and enjoy the affectionate esteem of all classes. They become the proud property of the nation and are known not only by the top intellectual crust, but by workers, farmers, and shopkeepers throughout the far reaches of the country. In no other European country is the sale of books, including volumes of poetry, as high in proportion to income and population figures as in Poland. Not even in France—and the French visitors are the first to admit it—exist so many brilliantly edited literary periodicals, enjoying as large a popular success as in Poland. It is as if the literary quarterlies and "little magazines" suddenly became the most sought-after publications in the U. S.

I watched Mariola and her partner slowly making their way back to our table. Like the majority of the girls in the place, she was dressed in a woolen skirt and a blouse. Her hair was shiny and well shaped. Even though they had been cut off from the centers of fashion for so long Polish women have somehow managed to retain a Western quality of taste in their clothes. In spite of the shabbiness of her dress, there was an air of distinction about her. In a room full of strong individual faces she had her own, definite personality; she was intelligent and disarmingly feminine—all at once. I had known Mariola for some time. A recent University graduate, now working for one of the large Warsaw weeklies, she was one of the attractive young "talkers" who made Warsaw such a stimulating city to be in.

"Here we think that it is not quite enough for a woman to be beautiful," a Polish novelist recently informed me; we were sitting in a Warsaw café discussing his recent trip to the U. S. "We also want her to have brains and talk well. What would there be left to do for a Pole once he got through making love?"

Because she had charm and could talk, Mariola was popular and admired.

Was she happy? She had never known "normal life" in our Western sense of the word. She had never lived without danger nor could she ever make any plans for the future. Now just 24 years old, she was six when the Germans occupied Poland. At eleven she lived through the nightmare of the Warsaw uprising—months of hunger, cold, hiding in cellars. Then came the era of Stalin; a suffocating, gray, hopeless time, a succession of school years overshadowed by distortion and lie. In October the shackles fell off. The new freedom—though limited and uncertain—was like a sudden illumination, like a blaze. But Mariola still has no material possessions to speak of; her room is a cubicle between curtains in an apartment shared with three other families; her food insufficient and poor; she hardly owns any clothes, knows no gay feminine frippery. Instead she is gifted with sharp wit, a capacity to work for fourteen hours or more, to laugh and talk well and to enjoy herself with a heady abandon, whenever the opportunity comes by.

Is this dynamic vitality a victory won over the circumstances of life under which she is forced to exist? Is it a way nature has to compensate for the uneven distribution of the material goods of this world? Yes, perhaps—but it is not full compensation.

"What would you like from life?" I have asked Mariola,

as I have several of her friends. The answer was always the same: "I would like to live *a normal* existence for a bit." By this they mean a family, a house or an apartment of their own, large enough to afford privacy, which so far has been an unattainable dream; money for the bare essentials of life, an occasional moment of leisure, but above all stability; no more political earthquakes for a while. They would like the present modest improvement in their lives to go on.

This almost pathetic desire for a spell of "normal existence" runs like a recurring refrain through Polish national life. Much has been said and been written about the current loosening of morals, about the atmosphere of "untrammeled sex" among youth, about the prevailing cynicism and nihilistic attitudes in the nation. They exist. War years, spent under the shadow of brute force, have taught the Poles realism. The Communist hypocrisy, the ever-present disparity between the word and the deed, injected cynicism into the romantically heroic approach which used to be a Polish tradition. Now the heroes are tired. They want peace. They are anxious to enjoy a steady, uneventful life for a while. But the prospects for stability are uncertain; although much has been gained since October, steps backward have also been taken. The game of jagged seesawing will go on creating tension and an atmosphere of a constantly shifting tomorrow. Hence frustration and a *carpe diem,* "let's enjoy ourselves while we may" attitude which slows down the country's march forward.

The vitality is there and the desire for freedom—more and more of it—never weakens. Contacts with the West are reopened: books, newspapers, scientific publications, magazines are now available in Poland. They are snapped up and read avidly. Each day the gap created by years of intellectual isolation gets narrower.

Though the young people I talked to are infinitely curious and anxious to hear about the West, they are also critical of what they call "the naively sentimental streak" in Western and, particularly, in American thinking. "Your people are so good and so wishfully non-thinking," a Polish journalist said to me. "I don't blame them. With the orderly existence you all lead, it is hard to understand the mentality of a people like ourselves who are continuously forced to face life at its basest." They are knowingly cynical, especially about authority of any kind. It is the sensual, down-to-earth novels of Ernest Hemingway and Graham Greene that appeal to young Polish readers, most of whom have seen too much of life to have many sentimental illusions left.

The young intellectuals are still searching. Their search will go on restlessly, but there is no more need to convince them of the superiority of Western culture; they know it. Even the Communist Party members in Poland came to this conclusion long ago.

It was time to leave Poland; time to return to my husband, my child and my work in the States. Over the antique telephone at the Bristol I talked to Denise, our 7-year-old girl, in New York and assured her I would be home in time for her birthday next week. I did not even attempt to call LOT. The line would be busy anyway; the airline booking office had only two telephones that worked; but I did not mind the inefficient procedure any more. By now I had come to know the LOT girls and their problems; we were friends. In a ramshackle little taxi, which seemed to be held together by pieces of string and scotch tape, I toured Warsaw, saying good-bye to official acquaintances and to friends. I walked along the Vistula Embankment and across, through the twisted streets of the Old City—among the gaily painted 17th-century houses put together from old drawings and maps. I remembered the Old City Square as I had seen it on the day after I arrived in Warsaw. It had then been softly bedecked by snow. Now there were boxes of begonias and crimson tulips in the windows and a flowering lilac bush in the courtyard of the house with the picture of *Syrena,* a Mermaid, Warsaw's emblem, on it.

I took a picture of charming, tree-lined Kubus Puhatek *(Winnie-the-Pooh)* street for Denise. When *Winnie-the-Pooh* was translated into Polish, the Warsaw children requested that a street be named to honor the beguiling little bear, whose introduction into their lives had thrilled them. Denise knows little about Poland, but one day I would like to take her there on a visit. Like so many Americans, she has a double heritage. It is a precious possession, one that gives an additional dimension to a life. I want her to be aware of it in the future. Will Poland be free and safe to return to? I uttered a fervent wish it be so.

Airplane travel these days creates an illusion of nearness, but it also makes the transition between two different worlds seem abrupt. One is always different in a different place and the speed of change leaves no time for the psychological adjustment of one's senses.

I left Warsaw's dilapidated airport at 6 P.M. on a rainy June evening. At eight o'clock the next morning Long Island Sound came into view and we swooped down for a New York landing. The magnificent span of the highways and the glistening opulent cars seemed fantastic after the muddy roads and the horsecarts of the land I had left less than twenty-four hours before.

In the doorway leading out of the customs shed stood my American husband, tall, calm, dependable and secure. Denise, our little girl, jumped into my arms happily.

"You must be absolutely exhausted," said my husband.

"I have never been more alive," I told him.